Partners in Planning
Information, participation
and empowerment

Susan B. Rifkin and Pat Pridmore

MACMILLAN

TALC

First published 2001 by
MACMILLAN EDUCATION LTD
London and Oxford
Companies and representatives throughout the world

www.macmillan-africa.com

ISBN 0–333–79266–1

10	9	8	7	6	5	4	3	2	1
10	09	08	07	06	05	04	03	02	01

This book is printed on paper suitable for recycling and
made from fully managed and sustained forest sources.

Printed in China

A catalogue record for this book is available from the
British Library.

Cover illustration by Victoria Francis

Acknowledgements

The authors and publishers wish to acknowledge, with thanks, the
following photographic and illustration sources:

Figure 1, Still Pictures/Mark Edwards; Figure 2, David Gifford;
Figures 4 and 6, The Hesperian Foundation; Figures 4 and 29,
The Mambo Press, Gweru, Zimbabwe; Figures 9, 10, 17, 18, 20,
24 and 26, IIED; Figure 39 Still Pictures/Christian Aid/Mauricio
Simonetti.

The publishers have made every effort to trace the copyright
holders, but if they have inadvertently overlooked any, they will
be pleased to make the necessary arrangements at the first
opportunity.

Acknowledgements

This book has had a long time in the planning stages. Using a participatory approach, we tried to consult as widely as possible to give this publication both form and substance. We are grateful to Dr David Morley, Professor Emeritus, Institute of Child Health and a Director of TALC who contributed the vision, the support and the follow through to see this book published. We are grateful to Shirley Hamber, of Macmillans for her encouragement and support for this project.

We would like to thank Pat Harman for help with the production of the book – for reading and commenting on the final draft and helping to find the various illustrations for the text. She encouraged us both to keep going when there appeared to be no light at the end of the tunnel.

Colleagues in the UK contributed comments, ideas and encouragement. We would like particularly to thank Indira Benbow-Biswas, Andrea Cornwall, Gill Gordon, Ruth Hope, Sally Hartley and Walter Salzer. In addition, comments and ideas from trainers who worked with participatory methods and approaches were greatly appreciated. We would particularly like to thank Martine Collumbien, Margaret Kaseje, Pauline Ong, Ben Osuga and Walter Salzer.

Hospitality, good humour and provision of space and quiet are necessary for good writing. St Julian's Retreat Centre, the Pridmore family and Sue and Peter Gibson gave us these necessary ingredients.

Finally, we owe a great big thank you to the participants of all our workshops, short courses and postgraduate classes in Europe, Asia and Africa who gave us the insight, experience and understanding to put this book together. We hope it will be a contribution and support for the work they are undertaking now and in the future.

Dedication

This book is dedicated to the many colleagues and students we have worked with around the world who have tailored our dreams of partnerships to the realities of life in poor and marginalised communities. It is especially dedicated to colleagues and students at the Tropical Institute of Community Health and Development in Africa (TICH) and the Director, Dr Dan Kaseje, who shared the vision of partnership, with special thanks and appreciation to James Omondi.

Contents

List of figures

List of abbreviations

AIDS	Acquired Immune Deficiency Syndrome
CAP	Community Action Plan
CHW	Community Health Worker
GTZ	Deutsche Gesellschaft für Technische Zusammenarbeit
HIV	Human Immunodeficiency Virus
KAP	Knowledge, Attitude and Practice
MCH	Mother and Child Health
NGO	Non-Governmental Organisation
PAR	Participatory Action Research
PET	Participatory Educational Theatre
PHC	Primary Health Care
PLA	Participatory Learning and Action
PR	Participatory Research
PRA	Participatory Rural/Rapid Appraisal
PID	Participatory Integrated Development
RA	Rapid Appraisal
RRA	Rapid Rural Appraisal
SARTHI	Social Action for Rural and Tribal Inhabitants of India
SWOT	Strengths, Weaknesses, Opportunities, Threats
TALC	Teaching Aids at Low Cost
TB	Tuberculosis
UN	United Nations
VIPP	Visualisation in Participatory Programmes
WHO	World Health Organisation
ZOPP	Goal Oriented Project Planning

Preface

There is now wide acceptance of the proposition that a participatory approach to needs assessment and programme planning produces information of real value, much of which could not be readily obtained by other means. This approach can also create knowledge that has more than local value. Poor communities can make a distinctive contribution to the knowledge base that should undergird national and international development policy and planning. The development policy agenda need no longer be defined exclusively by national policy makers, international agencies and bilateral donors; information and communication technology create the possibility for community-generated knowledge to influence such matters. Until poor communities have equitable access to international communication technology, the professionals who partner communities have an obligation to those communities to ensure this happens.

The 'Better World for All' report puts forward five sets of policy recommendations to reduce extreme poverty, and first among these is stronger voices and choices for the poor. Many conditions will have to be met for this to become a reality, and the poor people that constitute most of the world's communities will need partners. Three decades of experience with participatory methods in both industrialised and low-income countries have shown that with knowledgeable and skilful partners communities can gather the data and create the information they need to better understand the choices they should have, and to begin to claim those choices. It may be a counsel of perfection, but if every community of poor people was so empowered the world could be transformed and the forces of globalisation influenced to benefit rather than further impoverish poor people. In this book, health and educational professionals who aspire to be partners with communities' endeavours, but who are relatively new to participatory approaches to needs assessment and micro-level or locality planning, will find a compendium of tools essential to developing the knowledge base for community-controlled development.

The book rightly opens with a consideration of the importance of reliable and relevant information as a pre-condition to meaningful programme planning. Following the consideration of methods to generate information, the middle chapters of the book present a wide range of techniques in a very practical manner. The final chapters tie together all that has gone before, providing a framework for professional partners to successfully assist community leaders understand and apply a full range of information to design a programme that responds to the needs that have been jointly identified.

The real pleasure of this book will be for those who successfully practise the participatory methods and techniques it contains. To do so requires the not-so-common virtue of genuine professional humility, and the intention to accept and integrate the views of those who are often given little credit because of educational and/or economic status. Without this motivation the professional may still use the data-gathering methods described to uncover information useful for the professional's own purposes, but the process is unlikely to be one of empowerment for community members. And so it will not provide a sure base upon which to build effective, community-owned interventions that make the everyday life of poor people more productive and satisfying, which is what this book is ultimately about.

Hugh Annett
Head of the Health Department
Secretariat of His Highness the Aga Khan

Introduction

From experience

In a poor, dry area in the state of Gujarat in India a group of development workers came to help develop a programme which would improve the material and physical conditions of the women. The programme, called SARTHI (Social Action for Rural and Tribal Inhabitants of India), started by introducing a cooking stove which would reduce the smoke in dark airless cooking huts. From this small beginning local women formed themselves into a group of investigators. Working with programme staff, they began to look into the problems and needs of women in this area. Their needs assessment showed poor health to be the major problem. As a result a women's holistic health centre was set up to support a broad-based, holistic health programme. Local women were involved at all stages of planning the centre and the programme and in carrying out the activities. The health programme had three elements: 1) a maternal and child health programme, 2) participatory action research (PAR) on traditional medicines, and 3) gynaecological training through self-help. The health programme involved local women in empowerment workshops and activities in the community. It promoted empowerment by helping the women understand the extent and value of their own knowledge about traditional medicines and health practices. The women gained power and knowledge by understanding their use of local medicines and learning self-help practices. Programme planners and local women were equal partners in the needs assessment process. Both groups said that they had been transformed by it. By transformation they meant that they had become aware that women have fewer rights than men in their relationships and in society. This awareness led to them becoming more political in their outlook, and increased their commitment to change. The SARTHI programme is now being extended in response to the demands from other women who want to participate in it.

(*Source:* de Koning, K. and Martin, M. (1996) Participatory Research in Health, London: Zed Press.)

The above example of the SARTHI project shows us how professionals and local women who were poor and powerless did a planning exercise together in which both groups reached their goals. The professionals helped the women to improve their health. The women gained more than improved access to health care. They also gained the knowledge and confidence to expand on these improvements and to work together for social change. Wherever a participatory approach is used for planning the potential for empowerment exists.

FIGURE 1   A women's meeting to discuss child nutrition and family planning

Thinking about any type of planning, whether it is developing a neighbourhood support group or starting a health programme for the rural poor in Africa, the example given above can be very helpful. To summarise:

Information is **KNOWLEDGE**

Knowledge is **POWER**

Sharing knowledge is **EMPOWERMENT**

This book is about how to generate information for both knowledge and empowerment. The book has two purposes. The first is to explore how information can be used to develop equal partnerships between the professionals and the beneficiaries for programme planning. The beneficiaries are the people who are intended to benefit from a programme. The idea of partnership suggests an equal relationship between the professionals and the local beneficiaries. The second is to describe a number of techniques, share experiences and provide training exercises to help us develop the skills needed for these partnerships. This book presents a wide range of ideas on how to create and support partnerships. Below are definitions of some important terms used in this book.

- *Information:* Information means gaining facts about the things we need to know.
- *Knowledge:* By knowledge we mean interpreting and using information in a specific situation.
- *Generating information:* Generating information means the way information is collected, interpreted and used.
- *Empowerment:* Empowerment means creating opportunities and inspiration for those who are powerless. Empowerment is when the powerless gain the experience and confidence needed to influence the decisions that affect their own daily lives, and is the foundation on which partnerships must be built. Professionals cannot give power to those without power. Those who are powerless must take and exercise power for themselves.
- *We, us and our:* These terms are used to mean people who have education, training and experience to design, implement, monitor and evaluate programmes – in other words, the professionals.

Partners in Planning focuses on the partnerships we, as professionals, need to support for development programmes (particularly in the areas of health and education). It also looks at how we can keep these programmes going in situations where people are poor and powerless. The goal is to help professionals find ways to experience the value and potential of generating information and sharing decisions for programmes with lay people.

Programme planning carried out by professionals taking information from the beneficiaries (in our case the poor and powerless), and then interpreting this information themselves using their own professional experience is not partnership. Partnership means that beneficiaries are involved in the collection and interpretation of the information and in the decisions made on the basis of the interpretation. Experience shows that using a participatory approach provides opportunities for programmes to grow and carry on over time and helps people to become empowered.

Many books and journal articles have been written to help us understand the meaning of empowerment and to share experience. This book explores the idea and practice of empowerment through the way information is obtained and used. There are several reasons for this focus.

First, information is of major importance in today's world. Anthony

Giddens, the British sociologist and director of the London School of Economics, has suggested in his various articles and lectures that information has made it possible for us to see the world as a global village. Remote Muslim communities in the Himalayan foothills have now seen television. These communities scrape a living from poor agriculture and women farmers are given equal value to cattle. Yet men now meet in coffee houses to watch the latest episode of Dallas, the American melodrama about wealth and greed in Texas, USA. People in these communities want to wear Nike trainers, drink Coca-Cola and drive Cadillacs. Information speeding around the world by satellite has changed their wants and needs in less than a decade and the desires of the material world have begun to replace traditional values. Giddens also highlights the way in which the availability of information is critical to creating democracy in modern society. People are now better informed about their choices and are able to make better use of these choices, for example, when they decide how to vote.

Second, as stated at the beginning of this introduction, information is power. People who lack information, lack power and lack choices about how to improve their lives or control what happens to them. For example, if they do not have information about what makes them healthy or unhealthy they cannot act to improve their own health or avoid sickness. Although information alone does not guarantee change, it is needed before any change can take place.

FIGURE 2   The need for partnerships to encourage empowerment

People who have information have power and can make decisions to improve not only their own lives but also the lives of people who are poorer and less powerful than themselves. People who hold information may decide not to share their information. For example, bosses in work situations may decide what employees need to know and thereby keep control of their chances for promotion. Doctors who do not share information about health with their patients can make sure that people depend on them for curing disease.

Third, both the quality of information and the way in which it is generated is vital to starting up and developing programmes and keeping them going over time. Good quality information is the key to successful planning. The quality of information is improved when the beneficiaries give their own views and opinions about the programme rather than having another person speaking for them. Involving the beneficiaries in generating information also enables them to share in the ownership of the programme which is developed.

There are many examples of health or education development programmes that demonstrate the importance of involving beneficiaries in generating the information needed to plan programmes. Programmes that have been developed using information generated by the professionals only, frequently do not continue for very long after the professionals have left. This is because the professionals did not get enough accurate and useful information to design a good programme. It is also because they did not create a sense of ownership for the programme among the beneficiaries who therefore felt it was being imposed on them by the professionals. As a result the information product (the plan) and the process (the way in which the plan was developed) was no longer supported by the beneficiaries after funding and outside help was withdrawn.

This highlights the fact that information alone does not create partnerships. To repeat, partnerships are created through the process by which information is generated. If this process does not involve professionals and beneficiaries sharing information with each other then it does not lead to empowerment. Chapter 1 describes how the view that partnership is essential for successful planning has come about, and describes ways to support partnership.

Chapter 2 looks at methods that can be used to generate information. These methods are known as qualitative methods and they are used by planners and researchers who want to know how people view the world in which they live. These qualitative methods can be used together with other methods, known as quantitative methods, that tell us how many people might be affected by a problem. This chapter shows how professionals and community people can use both qualitative and quantitative methods to generate good information for programme planning.

Chapters 3 and 4 present a number of different techniques which can be used to generate information. These techniques are based on qualitative methods. They involve people in a participatory process, which promotes empowerment. We have selected the techniques that are most commonly used in participatory planning.

Chapter 5 presents a needs assessment exercise to introduce professionals to the benefits of participatory planning. This exercise has been used in countries as different as Tanzania and the United Kingdom. It has helped professionals to realise the value of participatory planning and gain experience to move from merely taking information from community people to supporting empowerment.

Chapter 6 looks at how the methods and techniques are used in an example of planning with partners which has developed in Kenya. This example shows how ideas presented in the previous four chapters can be used in a real life situation. In conclusion, it highlights the major challenges that professionals must meet when they choose to follow participatory approaches.

1 Why is information important for planning and empowerment?

This chapter presents an overview of planning and discusses how information can be generated so that it provides opportunities for people to become empowered. It starts by defining planning and showing how the process of information generation has changed in recent years. It explores the meaning of participation and then moves on to look at the conditions needed for participatory planning to develop. Finally it presents guidelines for participatory planning.

1.1 What is planning?

From experience:

Health planning in Zambia

CRISIS: The provincial medical officer receives a telephone call from his medical officer in a remote district. In one region of the district that is especially difficult to reach, the chief has reported an outbreak of cholera. Because the chief has a strong political position and some influence in the capital, the district medical officer has sent his vehicle with a few packets of rehydration fluid and his small supply of cholera vaccine to the area. However, the representatives of the chief are now in his office demanding more medicine and more attention immediately. The district medical officer has neither medicines nor vehicles to offer them. Can the provincial health office send a vehicle, more rehydration fluid and more cholera vaccine as soon as possible?

The above situation is real. One of the authors of this book was sitting with the provincial medical officer when he got the telephone call. In responding to the request, the provincial medical office was left with only one working vehicle, very few medical officers and almost no cholera vaccine. When another important demand for attention came through the next day, it was very difficult for him to provide help.

Andrew Green has written extensively on the planning process (see Further reading in Appendix 1). He explains that planning is a way of trying to ensure that the resources available now and in the future are used in the best possible way. Planning helps us to reduce uncertainty. If we know what resources are available and the priorities for using them, then we can decide how best to respond to crisis situations such as the one described above. More importantly, planning gives us a basis from which to decide what we want to achieve and what to do if we do not have enough resources to meet the needs. Planning also helps us to write down our objectives. These describe specific parts of a programme that are usually measurable. Objectives help us to relate the programme to the overall goal. The goal describes very broadly what we want to achieve. An example of a programme goal, an aim and some objectives are given below.

From experience:

Programme for promoting sexual health in Bombay, India

Goal: To promote the sexual health of young people living in a poor area of North Bombay in India.

Aim: To develop, implement and evaluate a peer-led sexual health education programme.

Objectives:
1 To raise awareness and gain support for the project from the community.
2 To carry out a participatory needs assessment for sexual health with young people from the community.
3 To enable young people, parents, head teachers, teachers and community leaders to develop educational activities and learning materials for sexual health.
4 To enable peer-educators to use the educational activities and learning materials to increase the knowledge and skills of their peers in school and out-of school.

To summarise, planning helps us to define our goal, aims and objectives and make detailed action plans. Action plans show how we can use our available resources (time, money and people) to achieve our objectives. Planning allows us to discuss, modify and review how we can best use limited resources and explain to others how we have made our decisions.

When we are planning we need to think about 1) political 2) administrative and 3) personal issues. These three issues determine whether or not we will be successful in reaching our objectives. The example of a crisis situation described at the beginning of this section highlights the way in which these three issues influence the response. In this example:

* What were the major political issues?
* What were the major administrative issues?
* What were the major personal issues?

If the district medical officer had thought about these issues before responding, he might have prevented the crisis at provincial headquarters.

We have now given a number of good reasons why planning is important. These include the value of a systematic way of identifying problems, setting priorities and developing action plans. Although planning does not automatically ensure that a programme will be successful it does give us a good start towards achieving our goals.

People have suggested that planning can be viewed as a series of steps, which provide a logical way to develop programmes. These steps make up a planning cycle. This information can be generated in a participatory or non-participatory way. In participatory planning, professionals and beneficiaries generate and share information at each step of the planning cycle.

FIGURE 3   The planning cycle

1.2   How has the way information is generated changed?

How, what and why we plan depends upon the information we generate. The importance of local people participating in collecting, interpreting, owning and acting upon information has only recently been recognised. A different view existed after the Second World War. In those days professionals thought that development could be achieved by so-called 'transfer of technology' from rich to poor countries. This included transferring information chosen by professionals in rich countries to people living in poor countries. The people who received this information were regarded as ignorant of the causes of their poverty. Programme planning was viewed as a job for professionals because they were the 'experts' on what information needed to be collected. It is now recognised that this view of development was not effective. There were many instances where the information transferred was ignored or rejected by the beneficiaries because it was not thought to be useful.

The ideas of Paolo Freire, the Brazilian educator, on adult education can help us to understand why this information was ignored or rejected. Freire called formal schooling, where a teacher gives information to students by lectures, the *banking* approach. He said that this approach treats people like objects or empty vessels to be passively filled up with information chosen and delivered by professionals. He argued that this way of providing information is deliberately used by the rich and powerful elites (including professionals) to keep the poor and powerless people down and oppressed. He called for an alternative *problem-posing* approach to education in order to reverse this situation. In this alternative approach learners are treated as active participants and subjects, rather than objects, of the learning process.

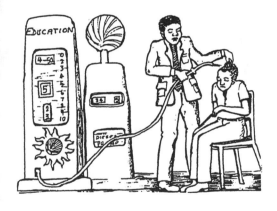

FIGURE 4   Two approaches to teaching and learning: *banking* approach and *problem-posing* approach.

Freire argued that through the development of *dialogue* between teachers and learners, the learners develop their ability to make decisions and to solve problems. This ability can help them to create a different and more equal society. Freire uses the term dialogue to mean a discussion between equals in a trusting environment in which people share ideas and experiences and together develop new understanding and awareness.

Freire spoke of *praxis* which for him is a process of 'reflection and action on the world in order to transform it'. For example, a father whose child dies from a preventable disease such as pneumonia may stop to reflect (think critically) about the reasons for his child's death. He may realise that the child died because he was too poor to buy the medicine the child needed and too powerless to get help. This new understanding could cause him to call together his neighbours and demand better health services.

Freire argued that in order to transform society and improve the lives of poor people the formal teacher and the learner needed to reflect in this critical way. In particular the teacher (whom he called the reformed oppressor) must join the learners (whom he called the oppressed) in their struggle for liberation.

Freire also spoke of *conscientisation* which can be translated as 'critical consciousness'. This means developing a deeper understanding of our own situation so that we can take action to change it. Freire argued that education which seeks to liberate the learners from their oppressive environment must start by increasing their critical awareness of the reasons why they are being oppressed. This awareness can help them become empowered to take action to improve their life.

This approach to education developed by Paolo Freire has made an important contribution to our understanding of the way in which generating information is a process rather than a product. In this process there is no fixed or standardised way of generating information. The important thing is to use a way that enables people to turn information and knowledge into power.

Participatory Action Research (PAR) has put the theories of Freire into practice. PAR builds on the experience of Kurt Lewin, an academic who studied the working conditions of automobile workers in the United States. He argued that their output improved if they were involved in looking for the reasons for poor working conditions and identifying ways to make improvements to these conditions. During the 1970s and 1980s Lewin's ideas were supported and expanded by the International Council of Adult Education. PAR is a type of research that involves everyone who is concerned with the research project, from the planning stage to final evaluation. It encourages the involvement of poor and powerless people who have traditionally been the objects and not the subjects of the research. Its main objective is to provide opportunities for these people to become empowered. PAR can be described as research that:

- is based on the belief that education should liberate people from oppression,
- is 'action oriented' in that the findings can be immediately used to take action,
- promotes the learning of both researcher and intended beneficiaries,
- is holistic in that it serves a broad range of community needs (such as health, social and economic needs) and raises critical awareness about the underlying reasons why people have these needs,

- is progressive in that it develops slowly over a period of time by constantly generating and interpreting information in order to decide what new information is needed.

In development programmes PAR has mainly been used to conduct participatory appraisals. Participatory appraisals are good examples of how the beneficiaries can be actively involved in planning programmes. These experiences are relatively new. Much of the early work was done because planners needed to get accurate information that could be quickly generated and used. To meet this need an approach called Rapid Rural Appraisal (RRA) was developed in the late 1970s by Gordon Conway and colleagues at the University of Chiang Mai in Thailand and also Robert Chambers (See Further reading in Appendix 1) and a group of colleagues at the Institute of Development Studies in Sussex, England. They developed RRA to improve the planning process in the field of agriculture and rural development. They believed that using RRA could help planners collect good information in a short time. (The survey methods they were using up to then were time consuming.) They also hoped that RRA could be used to overcome the biases or errors of the planners who were making decisions about programmes based on their limited contact with the people who were intended to benefit from the programmes. RRA was developed to help these planners get quick and accurate information using methods such as observation and interviews with so-called 'key informants'. 'Key informants' were community people with useful experiences to share. This information could then be used by planners to design programmes and activities.

Since the 1970s, the RRA approach has continued to develop and change as a result of increasing interest and experience in participation and empowerment. There is now great interest in the development of participatory methods that involve local people. Local people are no longer viewed only as providers of information about the local situation but rather as partners in generating, interpreting and using information. This broadening of participation has led to the term PRA being used for this more participatory approach to needs assessment. It has been used to mean Participatory Rural Appraisal, Participatory Rapid Appraisal and also Participatory Reflection and Action. These names are confusing because PRA actually takes a lot of time and it has been used in urban as well as rural areas. For this reason another term, PLA (Participatory Learning and Action), has most recently been used as an umbrella term to include all participatory approaches that seek to help people become empowered.

The main idea behind PRA/PLA is that generating information for planning is valuable as a step-by-step or systematic learning process in its own right and not only because it generates accurate information. By 'handing over the stick' or giving control of the information to be generated to the intended beneficiaries, both professionals and local people learn from and with each other.

Experiences of doing participatory appraisals have led to useful discussions about how information should be generated. Experiences have also raised some important questions for us to think about further. For example:

- Do professionals have the right attitudes and behaviour for developing partnership? (In other words do they show empathy, and value and respect local people's views?)
- Has the process of generating information merely taken information from people or has it created opportunities for genuine sharing and participation?
- Does an appraisal only need to be conducted once or should it be repeated at intervals during the life of a programme to support the empowering process?

Chapter 5 looks more closely at participatory appraisals. It uses them as an example of how generating information for a needs assessment can help people become empowered.

1.3 Why do we need to involve local people in planning?

In the past planning was done by the people who controlled resources and made decisions about how they were to be used. These people had no formal training in planning but they believed that their experience was what mattered

FIGURE 5   The expert and the farmers: 'Because you've done it successfully your way for generations, it doesn't mean it works.'

most. They believed that experience would overcome the problem of lack of formal qualifications. The people who planned development programmes were often 'outsiders' sent from donor agencies, the UN agencies or the World Bank.

Today views are different. Many technical schools and universities now provide courses for planners and managers. As a result there are increasing numbers of planning professionals, many of whom are educators, doctors and nurses. These courses can help to develop skills in the technical aspects of planning, such as cost-benefit analysis. However, they do not always help planners understand how professionals and beneficiaries think and relate to each other. Planning for the provision of health services provides a good illustration of the importance of understanding how the intended beneficiaries view the world. Professional planners may develop plans for health services that use the latest technology. They may be surprised when local people do not use these services because they are difficult to reach or are unfamiliar to them. Experience shows that in order to develop and implement a successful programme we need to involve all the local people who are intended to benefit from the programme as well as those who might be involved or in some way affected by it.

FIGURE 6

Some of the most important reasons for involving local people in planning are highlighted in The World Bank's *Participation Sourcebook* (see Further reading in Appendix 1):

1 Local people have a great amount of experience and insight into what works and what does not work, and why.
2 Involving local people in planning projects can increase their commitment to the project. The World Bank notes that verbal commitment alone does not ensure continued support for the programme. Only by developing a process where such commitment can be observed and supported can we gain continued support for the programme. Commitment is essential if the programme is to continue after donor funding stops, and make a sustained contribution to development.

From experience:

A school health project in Pakistan

A health action school project in Pakistan required schools to demonstrate their commitment by satisfying the following factors before being allowed to join:

i)   Commitment from senior management (headteacher) demonstrated by preparing a school development plan.
ii) Commitment from the staff (teachers and other school workers) demonstrated through consultation (agreement built during discussion meetings).
iii) Identification of two named teachers to prepare and carry out a yearly school health action plan linked to the school development plan to show how staff, pupils, parents, community leaders and health workers were going to be involved.
iv) An agreed way to release these two teachers to attend training workshops.
v)   Agreement to carry out a survey of what the school is already doing for health and a plan for demonstrating any changes made.

These factors were selected to allow the commitment of the school to be observed and supported by the planning team.

3 Involving local people can help them to develop technical and management skills and thereby increase their opportunities for employment. It also allows local people to become involved in making decisions about the development of a programme. This helps them gain some power and control over the programme and also over their own lives.

From experience:

Sexual health programme in Bombay

In a sexual health project in a very poor area of Bombay, India, young men and women from the local community are involved as research partners, working with project staff at all stages of the project cycle. They carry out participatory needs assessments and build on the results to develop learning materials and activities. They train peer educators in schools and in community groups to use these materials with their peers, and support them in their efforts. They monitor and evaluate the programme and share the experiences gained in workshops and seminars. In this way they help to develop and manage the programme and gain a wide range of skills which increase their opportunities for continued employment.

4 Involving local people helps to increase the resources available for the programme. Local resources are becoming increasingly important in programme development because both government and overseas aid is being drastically cut. Some people argue that relying on local resources relieves the government of its responsibility to people. However, the truth is that without local resources, fewer services and opportunities for improvement would be available to local people.

5 Involvement is a way to bring about 'social learning' for both planners and beneficiaries. 'Social learning' means the development of a partnership between professionals and local people in which each group learns from the other. Lay people learn how to collect and interpret information, write down priorities and manage programmes. Professionals learn how poor people, who are marginalised or excluded from society, view the world and how to translate this understanding into more successful development programmes.

From experience:

Effective community development through family participation in growth monitoring

In the 1980s research showed that the weight-for-age charts commonly used to monitor the growth and nutrition of babies and young children were not completed satisfactorily by the health workers and not used in making decisions about child feeding. A new method of weighing the child and recording the weight was then developed which allowed mothers to complete the growth chart themselves in their own homes. (This was called the Direct Recording Scale.[1]) Using this new method, a study in Kenya showed that 90 per cent of illiterate or semi-illiterate Maasai mothers were able to complete the chart and understand the process and its significance for their children. Their daughters and the infants' grandmothers also understood the meaning of the chart. This research highlights the gains that can be made by moving technologies out of the clinic into the family and community and enabling local people to learn by doing.

1.4 How do we view participation?

The ideas of Paulo Freire, and their use in Participatory Action Research, highlight the need for people who are poor and powerless to participate in programmes, which aim to improve their lives. To repeat, Freire's ideas help us to understand that participation is a *process*.

In the past participation has often been viewed as a *product*. This means that it has been used as a way to achieve success in programme activities. A good illustration of this view is the participation of people from the local community in disease control campaigns. For example, in the early years of the People's Republic of China local people killed rats and mosquitoes and dug ditches to bury the snails which spread schistosomiasis. Participation of this kind might be called mobilisation. It is an activity to *produce* control of communicable diseases.

In the 1980s and 1990s more work was done to explore the nature of participation as a process. For example, Norman Uphoff and J. Cohen have written the following questions to help us understand the nature of community participation:

- What kind of participation is occurring – in decision-making, in programme implementation, in programme benefits, in evaluation?
- Who is participating – local residents, local leaders, government people, foreign personnel?
- How is participation taking place – from above or below, voluntarily or with incentives, from which channels?
- What structures are there to support participation?
- How long has participation been going on for?
- Does participation help people participate in decision-making by building their experience and confidence?

Other people have helped us to understand better the links between participation and empowerment. For example, Peter Oakley has suggested that there are three categories or different types of participation:

- *Participation where local people are only involved in programme activities.* For example, local people may help to maintain an improved water supply system. This type of participation takes resources from people in time, labour, and possibly money. This type of participation does not promote empowerment.
- *Participation where local people help to decide what the priorities should be for the programme as well as being involved in the activities. However, professionals still control the overall aim of the programme.* For example, local people may participate in deciding that an improved water system is a priority and agree to maintain it. This type of participation is consultation. Professionals define both the problems and the solutions. Although they may modify these in the light of local people's responses they do not have to.

• *Participation where local people play an active and direct role in project development.* For example, local people do not simply accept the view of the professionals that an improved water supply is a priority. Instead, they participate in gathering and interpreting the information for a needs assessment. They participate in identifying problems and prioritising them, finding solutions, carrying out the activities and evaluating the activities. This type of participation allows local people to take control and develop a stake in maintaining the programme. It has great potential for enabling people to become empowered by providing opportunities for people who are poor and powerless to become involved in real choices about their own lives.

These three different types of participation can help us see participation as a *process* rather than a product. The aim of this process is to achieve specific activities that achieve the objectives of a programme. Several people have tried to illustrate participation as a process. For example, in 1969 Sherry Arnstein drew the ladder of participation shown in Figure 7. At the bottom of this ladder, participation is viewed as informing people about their rights and duties and at the top, it is viewed as giving citizens control of programmes.

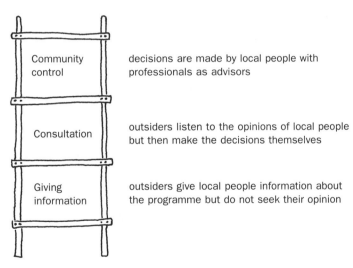

FIGURE 7   A ladder of citizen participation[2]

To link empowerment to participation, it is useful to view participation as a continuum. This continuum is shown in Figure 8. At one end of this continuum professionals take information from local people. At the other end, local people take full responsibility for the programme with professionals as resource people only.

A tool to help us understand how participation is always changing and to help us measure the process has been developed by Susan Rifkin, Wolfgang Bichmann and Frits Mueller. This tool, known as a spidergram, is described in Appendix 2.

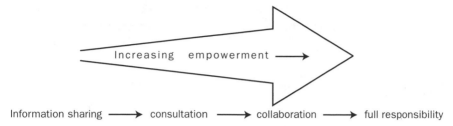

FIGURE 8   Participation for empowerment viewed as a continuum

1.5 How can we develop participatory planning?

When we help to plan programmes to improve people's living conditions we benefit greatly from the knowledge that local people have. It is not enough for us just to consult with local people. We need to turn our listening into learning so that we are able to find out what improvements are desired by and are acceptable to poor and marginalised people. We must allow local people to review their own situation. They must take control of and make decisions about development projects in their area.

The way in which participatory planning can be developed is described below:

- poor people begin as *receivers* of the programme benefits
- as they acquire skills and resources to demand and pay for services they become *clients* for these services
- and finally as they gain experience and confidence they become *programme planners and managers*.

This illustrates how the process of participatory planning can be empowering by allowing poor people to become the subjects rather than the objects of social development programmes.

> **Generating information** becomes
>
> **empowering** where
>
> **participatory climates** exist

The guidelines below help us develop partnership for participatory planning. These guidelines aim to turn the planning process into a learning experience not only for the professionals but also for the local people involved. This learning experience offers opportunities for empowerment, a major goal of all participatory approaches.

Guidelines for building partnerships in planning

1 Be concerned with both *content* and *process*.
  (*Content* means generating useful information. *Process* means involving local people.)
2 Be *systematic* and *flexible*.
  (*Systematic* means using a step-by-step approach. *Flexible* means being prepared to make changes.)
3 Develop *attitudes* and *behaviours* to promote partnerships.
  (This means demonstrating respect for and valuing the views of local people.)

1   Be concerned with both content and process

Let us first look at the *content*. Being concerned with the content means that we need to generate useful information so that we can create a programme, give it direction and monitor and evaluate it. Many planners believe that this information must be quantitative (providing numbers to tell us how much, how many, etc.). This often takes the form of a survey to find out what people think and what they do.

Those of us who are concerned with participatory planning believe that information for planning is of more value when it is not only quantitative but also qualitative. We are very concerned to have qualitative information because it can tell us how people involved in the programme view what is happening. It tells us how people view a situation and why they think this way. Collecting and analysing qualitative information is relatively new to many people involved in planning development programmes, particularly in the field of health. (The next chapter explores qualitative methods and their use for participatory planning.) Below is an example of how important qualitative information is. It shows how collecting only quantitative information led to a misunderstanding about people's knowledge of contraceptive methods.

From experience:

A family-planning survey in Nepal

A study undertaken by the World Fertility Survey in Nepal used a KAP (knowledge, attitude, and practice) questionnaire to measure the knowledge of rural women about contraceptive methods. In response to the question 'Have you heard about abortion?' nearly all the women said no. However, when two anthropologists talked to these women about contraception and asked them the same question all of the women answered yes. The anthropologists found out that the women had thought the question 'Have you heard about abortion?' meant 'Do you know how to perform an abortion?' The professionals who designed the KAP survey actually wanted to know whether the women knew of anyone who had had an abortion. The women had not interpreted the question in the same way as the professionals who designed the questionnaire.

(Adapted from Stone, L. and J.G. Campbell, (1984) 'The use and misuses of surveys in international development: an experiment from Nepal', *Human Organization*, Vol. 43, No. 1, pp. 27-37.)

Now let us look at *process*. Being concerned with process means that we need to involve the beneficiaries in planning the programme. To build partnerships we must make sure that the way in which information is generated develops and supports a process in which professionals and local people share their knowledge and experiences. For example, in a participatory needs assessment local people and professionals may walk through the community together, generating and writing down the information needed for planning. After the walk they can use this information to draw a transect diagram and show it to the whole community to share what they have learned and to add more information to the diagram. (Transect diagrams are presented in more detail in Chapter 3.) It is this process of generating and analysing information and sharing learning which makes planning participatory and helps programmes to continue for many years. (Some guidelines to help develop this process are provided later in this chapter.)

2 Be systematic and flexible

As professionals and planners it is important for us to be open and flexible to new ideas and new situations. We need to learn how to spend time with local people in places where they feel most comfortable, such as the market place or community centre, and to interact in a less formal way. We also need to listen and be open to new ways of thinking about problems and ideas – and willing to explore them. However, this does not mean being disorganised. A systematic (step-by-step) approach is important.

The objectives of the programme should be written down and an action plan to reach these objectives should be prepared. We also need to know whether the objectives have been achieved. The objectives need to include statements about the outcomes of the programme (what is to be achieved – for example, increased use of oral rehydration fluids for treating diarrhoea) and the process (using participatory approaches).

To help us develop a systematic approach to planning the following six questions are useful:

- **What?**

What is the purpose of the planning exercise? We need to describe this clearly and to write down the intended outcomes. If one of our objectives is to build partnerships and promote empowerment then this objective needs to be clearly written down.

- **Why?**

Why are we – the professionals – undertaking this planning exercise? If we have already identified the issue we are interested in then we must be open and honest about it and state this clearly from the outset. For example, if we have funding to improve the nutrition of children from 1-5 years old, then we need to tell people that this is the situation.

From experience:

What and Why? An example from India

What?
The purpose of the planning exercise is to involve young research partners from the community working with project staff, to carry out a participatory needs assessment to identify the sexual health needs of young people in the Bhandup area of Bombay.

Why?
The needs assessment is being done to allow young research partners to develop a health education programme to improve the sexual health of young people in the area.

These two questions – What? and Why? – are vital to developing a systematic (step-by-step) approach to planning. The answers to these two questions need to be clearly understood by the professionals and the beneficiaries involved in the programme. Many programmes have failed because these questions have not been answered clearly, mainly because the people involved had different expectations for the planning process. For example, we may ask the beneficiaries to identify any problems and issues they have in relation to the development of their community. If we already know that we are only prepared to support a programme that prioritises sexual health or water and sanitation and do not tell local people about this, then we are misleading the community. Such experience reduces the willingness of local people to believe what we say and leads to suspicion and mistrust. It also makes local people reluctant to be involved in future programmes.

• **Who?**

Who is intended to benefit from the programme and who else might be involved or in some way affected by it? The answer to this question will help us to identify a list of people who are known as the stakeholders in the programme. This list should include the names of people who:

• have professional skills to plan and implement the programme
• are intended to use and benefit from any services or outcomes that the programme has identified. These people are called beneficiaries but they are also known as the programme 'target group'. In development programmes these are mainly people who are poor, marginalised and socially excluded from the community
• are directly affected by the programme but who are not intended to use the services or outcomes. These people may be government officials and others employed by local authorities and NGOs which relate to the programme
• have influence and power that they might use to harm the programme if they are not involved at the beginning. These people include the informal leaders in the community.

• **Where?**

Where will the programme take place? The answer to this question will provide us with a detailed description of the geographical location in which the programme is to be carried out. It will identify which communities are to be included as well as the actual location of the programme activities.

From experience:

Who and Where? Example from India

Who?
The beneficiaries are young people aged 15 to 24 years old in Bhandup. Other people involved or affected by the programme are the parents and schoolteachers of these youths, the community-based youth group leaders, health workers and women's groups.

Where?
The needs assessment will be conducted with community-based groups in Bhandup.

• **When?**

When will the programme be carried out? The answer to this question will provide a detailed timetable or plan of activities. This timetable will take into account the resources available, and what it is practically possible to do.

• **How?**

How shall we carry out the planning exercise? This involves writing down a detailed plan by which the objectives are going to be met. For participatory planning we need to think carefully about how to involve local people so that we meet both of our objectives 1) to generate information and 2) to develop shared learning between professionals and local people.

From experience:

When and How? An example from India

Participatory needs assessment	Jan	Feb	Mar	Apr
Assist community youth groups to select 25 young research partners.	XXXX			
Prepare and conduct workshop to train needs assessment team in participatory methodology.		XX		
Pilot (try out) participatory techniques.			X	
Conduct participatory needs assessment to find out the sexual health needs of different youth groups.			XX	
Write needs assessment report and share the findings with community partners.				X

(X = 1 week)

The example given above shows that one way we can meet both of these objectives is to design training workshops to help us as professionals and planners develop the attitudes and behaviours we need to work with local people in a participatory way. Some good ideas about how to plan and manage these workshops can be found in the books *Participatory learning and action: a trainer's guide* by Jules Pretty and his colleagues and *Health Care Together* by Mary Johnston and Susan Rifkin (see Further reading in Appendix 1). Planners will also have to choose which methods and techniques to use to meet the two objectives given above. In the next chapter we discuss the range of methods and techniques which are commonly used to promote participatory planning. The example opposite shows how important it is that we choose the method or technique that is *most useful* for helping us to meet our objective.

From experience:

Focus groups on HIV/AIDS in Africa

A doctor who had spent many years in Uganda saw the rapid spread of HIV and an increase in AIDS and wanted to help to curb it. He decided on two courses of action. His *first objective* was to do some research to find out how big the problem was while his *second objective* was to educate people about the danger of HIV and the way in which it is spread. He decided to use the group interview method to find out how big the problem was and during these interviews he told people about the dangers of the disease and the way it is spread. Although he conducted over 80 group interviews he was not able to generalise or extend his findings to a larger population. In addition, he could not be effective as a health educator because giving people health information on its own was not an effective way to help them avoid HIV. Consequently he failed to achieve his goal of curbing the spread of HIV/AIDS. He could have saved himself a lot of time, trouble and money if he had thought more carefully about his objectives and the best methods to achieve these objectives. He might have been more effective if he had involved people in role-plays and discussions to explore attitudes to HIV and help develop life skills (such as negotiation and decision-making skills) and improve their access to sexual health services and products.

3 Developing attitudes and behaviours to promote partnerships

To form partnerships for planning, professionals need to understand how to work with people who have different cultural and educational backgrounds and experiences from theirs. Robert Chambers, who has written many books and articles about participation, suggests that to build the type of partnerships needed for participatory planning we need to think about three key issues, which he calls the three pillars of participation. These pillars are:

- Methods
- Behaviour and attitudes
- Sharing.

Methods
It is essential for us to use participatory methods and techniques. The next three chapters look at methods and techniques.

Behaviour and attitudes

The training and experiences that we have as professionals are often barriers to creating a good feeling between us and people who do not think the same way we do. For example, a health worker who is trained to exercise authority over patients, to give injections, prescribe drugs and deliver health messages, such as 'boil water, wear shoes, wash hands and eat a balanced diet', may find it difficult to spend time learning with and from local people. We need to overcome these barriers and help to build bridges between the different ways professionals and local people view the world. Some guidelines for developing partnerships are shown below.

Guidelines for developing useful attitudes and behaviours for supporting partnerships

1 Give respect to those who are generating information. Recognise in your mind and in your speech and actions the importance of their contribution.
2 Develop skills as a good listener. Try to understand what is being said, not what you want to hear.
3 Be positive. Look for good points which people make and acknowledge this contribution.
4 Be open to new ideas.
5 Act as a facilitator to help people share experiences and learn from each other. Do not act as an expert or pass judgement on information generated by local people. Acknowledge the information and probe it, but do not correct it. Do not lecture people and do not interrupt when someone else is talking.
6 Give feedback on what has been discovered or learned to those people who have generated information. For example, if children have been drawing pictures and writing about what makes them healthy, ask their permission to display the pictures to the whole group and discuss the information generated. This exchange provides an extra opportunity for interaction and helps motivation and learning.
7 Be relaxed and open. Try to meet community people at a time that is convenient for them. Be prepared to work long hours and stay in the community.
8 Recognise the need to find ways of continuing to support the process of participation throughout the entire planning process.

Training exercise:

Developing useful behaviour and attitudes

Purpose: To develop good relationships between professionals and local people.

Time: 45 minutes.

Materials: None

Steps:
1 Explain that if project workers believe they are better than local people then they are likely to behave in a superior way towards them. This leads to unequal partnership, where local people are dependent on project workers or even hostile towards them. Unfortunately this is a very common situation in the 'helping' professions. In this situation project workers do things *for* local people rather than *with* them. The unspoken message is that local people cannot do things for themselves – so they do not.
2 Explain that they are going to do a 'fishbowl activity' to look at how project workers can develop friendly relations with individuals or groups in the community. It is called a fishbowl because some participants will do a role play in the centre of the room and the other participants will sit around them in a circle to observe.
3 Ask participants to sit in a circle and place some chairs or mats on the floor in the centre. Invite about six participants to role play members of the community peer group, who have had little schooling, and ask them to sit on the chairs or mats. Brief one participant (preferably in advance) to role play an insensitive project worker having a meeting with the community for the first time to identify problems the project worker is having. You can develop the brief for the insensitive project worker by asking him or her not to follow any of the guidelines for developing partnerships shown on page 29. Ask the remaining participants to observe the role play carefully.
4 Run the role play of the meeting and then ask the observers: 'What did you see happening that hindered the establishment of friendly relationships between the project worker and the community group?'
5 Explain that the same role play will be run again, but this time participants can stop the role play by clapping their hands, whenever they see an opportunity to improve the rapport between the project worker and the community group.
6 Run the role play again and each time someone claps their hands ask them to come and show the group how they think it could be

improved. (This technique is known as Forum Theatre and we will describe it more in Chapter 4.)

7 Ask the observers: 'What did you see happening which helped to establish friendly relationships between the project worker and the community group?'

8 Write their replies using a thick pen.

Sharing

To work in partnership with local people we need to recognise and value the sharing that takes place. Through this sharing, local people learn new skills and new ways of seeing their world from professionals. Professionals not only learn new information about the community, but also learn how the community views their situation and how they define problems and see solutions to these problems.

As professionals we have skills in using a systematic, step-by-step approach to the collection of information. Local people have skills in generating information that is useful and accurate. Both types of experiences are valuable and need to be shared. Local people are often able to collect information from those who either distrust professionals or might tell professionals what they think they want to hear. By working together as partners, professionals and local people generate better and more truthful information.

Another way of sharing is through interpreting the information generated together. Professionals help local people gain experience in generating information and local people interpret and share their findings with the professionals. For example, professionals may help local people to develop flow charts to explore the causes and consequences of teenage pregnancy in their community. These charts are then shared with the professionals and discussed to increase the learning. (We will look at flow charts in Chapter 4.)

This process of sharing raises a very important question about the use and value of this information. The question is: 'Who owns the information?' We know that the information generated is a contribution from everyone involved in the process. This process begins with shared information generation and moves on to shared interpretation and finally to shared decision-making. However, professionals have often taken ownership of the information at the generation stage and used it as they judged best. There are many examples where professionals, claiming to build partnerships, have taken information and used it to promote their own interests. It is important to raise this question about ownership and use of information, because it needs to be discussed and agreed upon from the start by all those involved in the planning process. If there is no agreement on ownership it can easily become a point of disagreement and undermine all previous attempts to strengthen participation and develop partnership. An example is provided opposite to illustrate a way of encouraging community ownership of the information.

From experience:

A community-based nutrition programme in Kenya

A community-based nutrition programme run by the Ministry of Culture in Kenya uses the approach know as PLA (Participatory Learning and Action) to involve community members in generating, analysing and using information for planning community programmes. At each stage of the planning process information is collected in visual form, such as maps and diagrams which are drawn on the ground and then discussed by the whole group to increase the learning. After this discussion two copies of each diagram are made on thick paper. One copy is kept by the community and the second copy is kept by the planning team. The copy in the community is used by community members to guide community action and to share their knowledge and experiences with visitors from other communities and from local and central government.

Guidelines for helping us to develop partnerships

1 Listen carefully.
2 Act as a facilitator to help people generate and share information.
3 Give feedback by regularly telling participants what has been learned.
4 Support the participatory process.

Notes

1 Direct Recording Scales are available through TALC, P.O. Box 49, St Albans, Herts AL1 5TX, UK.
2 Adapted from Arnstein, S. (1969) 'Eight rungs on the ladder of citizen participation', reprinted in: Cahn, E. and Passett, B. (eds) *Citizen participation: effecting community change*, New York: Praeger.

2 Choosing methods and encouraging attitudes and behaviours that promote partnerships

This chapter, and the following two chapters, describe the main methods and techniques for involving local people in generating and analysing information. A technique uses one or more methods. The need to be systematic and make sure our information is valid by cross-checking is stressed. Cross-checking means comparing information on the same issue, which has been generated in different ways, in order to see how well it matches. Each method and technique is discussed in turn, starting with a description of each and how it is used. An example is given from experience and then a training exercise is presented to practise skills needed.

2.1   Choosing the best method

Information generation requires some specific skills. We, as planners and professionals, will need to gain these skills ourselves and also help intended beneficiaries of the programme to gain them. Too often people think that involving local people means merely asking them to come to meetings or talking to them about their ideas. Experience suggests this is not enough. We need to develop a systematic way to generate information which everyone involved in the planning process can use. If we do not do this then we get poor information. For example, an unskilled planner may ask a question such as 'Don't you think you need more teachers here?' This question is called a leading question because it leads the person answering the question to give a response that supports the planner's view. This response may not truly reflect the person's view. Another example is when the planner asks a question but only listens to the information she or he wants to hear.

We can use two methods to understand how people view their world and to help involve them in programmes that respond to their needs. These two methods are 1) quantitative and 2) qualitative.

Quantitative methods are designed to help us measure things so we can see how big a need or problem is. These methods are used in scientific experiments for testing ideas or hypotheses. Quantitative information can provide us with a broad view about a problem. It is usually generated as numbers and helps us to answer questions like – *how much, how many, how often*? For example:

• How many mothers breastfeed their children for at least two years?

- How much weaning food do they give?
- How many times a day do they give it?

This sort of information is often obtained through carrying out surveys. It can be very precise and accurate. It can be analysed using statistics. It produces evidence that can be used to build a strong argument for the presence of a problem and to link the problem with a cause. It also allows us to make generalisations. Generalisations mean that we can assume the evidence from the sample used in the survey can be used to meet needs or seek solutions for large numbers of people.

Qualitative methods are designed to help us find out how individuals or groups look at the world around them. They can help us build up a deeper understanding about what people think. They can also help identify local concerns, opinions and beliefs and provide detailed information on important issues. We can use qualitative information to:

- Develop good questions for a quantitative survey.
- Increase our understanding of the reasons why a problem is linked to a particular cause (as discovered by the quantitative survey). For example, in one area of Botswana, a quantitative survey showed that dehydration caused by diarrhoea was a major cause of death in babies. Qualitative information, from focus group discussions, revealed that many mothers believed dehydration could only be treated by a traditional healer 'who makes a cross on the "soft-spot" (fontanelle) on the baby's head'.
- Involve intended beneficiaries in generating information and in planning programmes.

Qualitative information is usually collected by talking to people. The information generated in this way is quickly interpreted to help us decide what further information we need. This approach to information gathering is said to be 'iterative' because it involves asking the same question many times to different people in order to gain a variety of views. In this way we can build up a better picture of how things work. Qualitative information helps us to understand what people think about their situation and their problems and what is most important to them. It answers questions such as 'What are your views about .....?' For example:

- What do mothers think about weaning foods?
- What do mothers think about breastfeeding?

In the past, people have argued that qualitative and quantitative methods cannot be used together because they answer different questions. However, experience continues to suggest that better projects are developed when both methods are used to generate information for planning. The example below gives us ideas on how we can use the two methods together.

From experience:

Investigations about HIV/AIDS

Quantitative methods have been used to show how AIDS (Acquired Immune Deficiency Syndrome) has increased, where most cases are to be found, and who is most at risk. However, quantitative methods have not been able to tell us much about how people believe they can get AIDS or what behaviours people think promote the spread of AIDS. We know that HIV (the Human Immunodeficiency Virus, which causes AIDS) is linked to sexual behaviours and information about these behaviours is very sensitive. Using qualitative methods, researchers have been able to discover how people think AIDS is spread. For example, in Swaziland research showed that people thought AIDS could be caused by shaking hands with, or drinking from the same glass as someone who has AIDS. Health education programmes are now being designed to address problems based on this information. Both quantitative and qualitative information have been important in promoting AIDS awareness and lowering the spread of the disease.

The strengths of each method are summarised below. *The important question is how to choose the right method for the problem under investigation.*

The strengths of and differences between qualitative and quantitative methods

1 Quantitative methods change the situation to test how it might be. Qualitative methods study the situation as it is.
2 Quantitative methods test an idea or hypothesis. Qualitative methods describe a situation.
3 Quantitative methods see a situation as a sum of all its parts and examine a cause and effect relationship. Qualitative methods see a situation as more than a sum of its parts and examine the relationship of all of the parts.
4 Quantitative methods record information in numbers choosing specific aspects of that situation. Qualitative methods record information in words or pictures by collecting data recording people's experiences and not selecting any pre-chosen aspect.
5 Quantitative methods stop the researcher from having any personal involvement with the human subjects. Qualitative methods involve the researcher so he or she can gain understanding of how people think.
6 Quantitative methods seek to look at change by measuring

outcomes (what is achieved) and impact (what effect it has). Qualitative methods pay attention to process (how things change).

7 Quantitative methods seek to generalise or extend their findings. Qualitative methods assume each case is special and seek to capture the way in which it is special.

8 Quantitative methods claim to be neutral or not prejudiced. Qualitative methods use the researcher's personal insight and understanding to examine a situation but not to judge it.

9 Quantitative methods develop a technique such as a questionnaire and then use it for getting information. Qualitative methods often change the technique used during the study as new understanding is gained and/or the situation changes.

2.2   How do we use qualitative methods for participatory planning?

Generating information for partnerships uses both quantitative and qualitative methods. In an earlier book, *Partners in Evaluation*, Marie-Therese Feuerstein described the use of quantitative methods for participatory planning. This chapter examines how we can use qualitative methods. Qualitative methods can be used to generate information for planning a programme and also to generate information on the planning process.

To repeat, qualitative methods are designed to help us understand how people think about the world they live in. These methods come from the discipline known as anthropology. Michael Patton has described qualitative methods as 'people-oriented'. By this he means they seek information that is rich in detail and helps us understand what people believe and think. This information is subjective and impressionistic but, when collected systematically, it can give findings that are as reliable and trustworthy as those based on quantitative information. Qualitative methods have made a valuable contribution to the development of participatory planning for development programmes.

Qualitative methods are people-oriented methods because:

- They help us find out what actually takes place among people and what people say about the situation.
- They let us get close enough to the people and the situation we are concerned with to understand personally what is really going on.
- They include a great deal of description of people, activities, exchanges and settings.
- They allow information to be provided to solve problems and generate ideas.

Qualitative methods allow us to:
- investigate a process to see how ideas and actions have changed over time and why this change has taken place,
- investigate meaning and understand how people see their world and why they use different strategies to deal with that world,
- have the principal investigator(s) (manager, resource holder, decision maker) work closely with the people who are intended to benefit from the programme,
- gain 'hands-on' experiences in working with partners in the field rather than reading reports others have written,
- allow intended beneficiaries of a programme to become part of the process for information generation.

Below is an example of how qualitative methods can be used to improve the situation of poor, marginalised people.

From experience:

A family planning project in Rwanda

A family planning project in Rwanda wanted to develop a programme to address the needs of single mothers. Project workers interviewed these mothers and discovered that the society in which they lived disapproved of single mothers and consequently gave them little support. In addition, fathers felt little responsibility for their children. Most single mothers were poor. One result was that the children were malnourished. Another was that the women often turned to commercial sex work to buy essential items such as food, soap and medicine. Because these women were unmarried they were denied access to family-planning services and therefore more unwanted children were often born. In the interviews these mothers discussed their problems freely with the project workers who were thereby able to build up a better picture of the conditions in which the women lived. Through these discussions, the project workers and mothers were together able to find ways of changing the family planning programme to meet their expressed needs better.

(Adapted from B. Maier, R. Gorgen, A.A. Kielmann, H.j. Diesfeld and R. Korte (1994) *Assessment of the District Health System using qualitative methods*, London: Macmillans).

The most important qualitative methods are *interviews* and *observations*. In addition, we look at documents to help us cross-check our information. We can also use techniques that generate information in a visual form (as writing on cards and/or pictures), to encourage participation and to enable local people to have more opportunities to become empowered. Visualisations are discussed in detail later in the chapter.

2.3 Conducting interviews

What are interviews?

An interview is a meeting between two or more people to discuss a topic chosen by the person who is conducting the interview. The person conducting the interview is known as the interviewer and the person or persons being interviewed are the respondents. Interviews can be:

FIGURE 9   Interviewing

- *Structured* where the exact wording and sequence of questions are determined in advance and all the respondents are asked exactly the same questions in the same order.
- *Semi-structured* where the interviewer has a set of guidelines but the exact topics and the order in which they follow depends on the interview situation.
- *Unstructured* or *narrative* where the questions emerge from the interview and follow the order in which the respondent talks about them. The questions, wording or topics are not decided upon before the interview.

To be able to conduct good interviews we need to keep the following points in mind:
1 We need to have good communication and listening skills. Before we begin to interview people it is a good idea to spend some time finding out about our own strengths and weaknesses and trying to improve our skills.

Training exercise:

Improving communication and listening skills

1 Ask participants to go into groups of three to practise communication and listening skills. In each group there is a speaker, a listener and an observer.
2 Ask the speakers to talk for two minutes on a subject of their own choice to do with work. Ask the listeners not to talk except for a few encouraging words, and not to take notes. Ask the observers to watch carefully the behaviour of the speaker and the listener.
3 After two minutes, stop the speakers and ask the listeners to repeat in their groups as much as they can remember. Then ask the observer to comment on what was incorrect, forgotten or added.
4 Ask the participants to change places within their groups and repeat the exercise until all members of the group have had a turn to speak, listen and observe. (Each speaker chooses a new topic.)
5 Ask participants to discuss the following questions in the small groups.
   What helped me to listen?
   What hindered my listening?
   What hindered my remembering?
   What did I learn about myself as a listener?
   How did the speaker know that the listener was listening?
6 Lead a discussion with the whole group taking feedback from each small group and listing their responses to the questions on the flipchart.

You will find more information and exercises in the following books: *Health Care Together* by Johnston and Rifkin; *Participatory Learning and Action* edited by Pretty and his colleagues; *Training for Transformation* by Hope and Timmel. (See also Further reading in Appendix 1.)

2 We need to build a good atmosphere with the respondents to encourage an open and honest exchange of information. As we discussed in Chapter 1, to help develop this atmosphere we need to show attitudes that support sharing. Our body language (the way we sit or stand and our facial expressions) needs to show that we are interested and friendly towards the respondent. We need to be careful not to express our own values or to pass judgement on the respondent's views. We also need to make sure that the interview is being done in a place which is comfortable and relaxing, both for the respondents and for ourselves. Doing interviews with people in their

own homes or in the places where they go for relaxation helps to create this atmosphere.

FIGURE 10   Be a good listener

The guidelines below are important for making an interview successful. Interviews can be done individually (with the interviewer and one respondent) or they can be done with groups of respondents. It is useful for the person conducting the interview to take a colleague with them who can observe the communication during the interview.

Guidelines for conducting an interview

Preparation:
1 Make sure the purpose of your interview is clear.
2 Make a short checklist of topics or questions (four or five are enough) to guide the interview.

Introduction:
1 Always introduce yourself at the start of the interview.
2 State clearly the purpose of your interview.
3 Ask the respondent if he or she has time to discuss the topic with you at the moment or to suggest another time that is convenient.
4 Explain that your conversation will be confidential.

Conducting the interview:
1 Begin with some friendly general conversation to help the person feel at ease.
2 Then ask a question which is easy for the respondent to answer. Do not begin with a personal question, it may cause offence and stop the free flow of information.
3 Only express one idea in each question to avoid confusing the respondent.

4 Avoid questions where the respondent only needs to answer yes or no because that can stop the flow of information.

5 Do not ask 'Why?' very often because it can make the respondent feel anxious or angry.

6 Beware of asking questions that try to influence the respondent's answers. For example, never ask 'Don't you think that ...?' This is called a leading question.

7 Avoid using negative questions such as 'Do you think that people should not .....?' These questions can confuse the respondent.

8 Be sure that you have clearly understood the answer. If not, ask the respondent to repeat the answer. Always ask the respondent to explain words and ideas that you do not fully understand. Do not assume that you know what the answer is because of your own knowledge and experience.

9 Avoid passing judgement, giving advice or your own opinion.

10 Tell the respondent when you are going to change the topic so that the respondent can be prepared.

11 Avoid discussions that are not useful. Keep to the topic of the interview.

12 Watch your body language as it tells the respondent what you are feeling and can help or disturb the interview.

Closing the Interview:

1 Keep the interview short. Interviews rarely last more than one hour and most last only 45 minutes.

2 Summarise the main points as you have understood them and ask the respondent if your summary correctly reflects what was said.

3 Ask the respondent if there are any questions he or she would like to ask you.

4 Thank the person for their time and trouble.

Providing feedback is important. Decide how you are going to let the respondents know the results of your interview.

Guidelines for recording an interview

1 Use a discreet notebook.
2 Record the detail of what is said in the language used.
3 Record body language and feelings expressed.
4 Record observations and how the interview went.
5 Record who said what and whether others agreed.
6 Make follow-up notes after the interview with the observer.
7 Record personal impressions.

Remember you must allow time to transcribe your material. It will take you about twice as long to transcribe as it took you to do the interview.

Individual interviews

These have the advantage that:

- Topics can be explored in more depth.
- Questions can be more focused and relevant.
- New topics can be identified and explored.
- Topics in structured and semi-structured interviews can be approached systematically and responses can be more easily organised and interpreted.
- The interviewer can more easily respond to the situation.

The disadvantages include:

- Important topics might be left out because neither the interviewer nor the respondent has thought about these topics.
- The interviewer might change the order and wording of topics in unstructured and semi-structured interviews. This could change the answers.

From experience:

Individual interviews

Researchers in Australia conducted individual interviews with men 24-37 years old who were infected with HIV (Human Immunodeficiency Virus) to find out how they felt about their condition. The researchers were well trained, experienced interviewers who showed sensitivity and guaranteed confidentiality. Thirty men were willing to share their views. The interviews were tape-recorded. The information generated showed how being HIV positive made it difficult for the men to feel at ease with themselves either physically or morally. It also showed what a bad effect their HIV status had on their relationships with other people. The way that local people viewed them made it difficult for them to receive health care and lowered their self-esteem.

(Adapted from B. Maier, R. Gorgen, Kielmann, A.A. Diesfeld, H.j. and Korte, R. (1994) *Assessment of the District Health System using qualitative methods*, London: Macmillans.)

Training exercise:

Individual interviews

Purpose: To provide opportunities to develop an interview guideline and the skills needed to conduct individual interviews.

Time: One and a half hours: 20 minutes preparing interview guide, opening statement and questions; 5 minutes interview each for three people; 10 minutes feedback per person for three people; 5 minutes feedback per group; 15 minutes whole group concluding discussion.

Materials: Notebooks and pens/pencils.

Steps:
1 Explain the purpose of the session. Ask the participants to work in groups of three and to give each person the opportunity to be an interviewer, a respondent and an observer.
2 Ask each group to produce their own interview guide to explore a topic that the respondent will have some knowledge about. (Good topics might be their opinion on a current event or a problem that is shared by all those participating in the training.)
3 Tell them to develop an opening statement that tells the respondent the purpose of the interview, and to draft one or more opening questions to start the interview.
4 Ask them to decide who will be the interviewer, respondent and the observer and how they are going to rotate these roles.
5 Tell them they have 5 minutes to conduct the interview and ask them to start.
6 After 5 minutes stop the interviews. Ask groups to feedback to each other by asking the interviewer to say how he or she felt about the interview and to identify his or her own strengths and weaknesses. Ask the respondent to give feedback on what the interviewer did well and on how they could improve their skills. Ask the observers to give feedback on the interactions.
7 Repeat this exercise until each person has been in each role. Each person should make notes of the main strengths and weaknesses demonstrated by the interviewers.
8 Lead a general discussion about the experience.

Group interviews

In a group interview, the group can consist of between 4-12 people. An interviewer (known as the moderator) facilitates the discussion. The interviewer generally uses four or five questions to guide the discussion, but allows the conversation to range freely around these questions. Another person records the interview and makes notes of the way people in the group interact with each other. Group interviews provide us with the chance to find out how much difference there is in beliefs about a given topic. These discussions help us to decide how well ideas and health messages are accepted, and to understand why they may be rejected. Group interviews also help us to find out how information is passed on.

Group interviews have the advantage that:
- They enable a great deal of information to be gathered in a short period of time.
- The respondents build on each other's ideas.
- They allow respondents to exchange ideas with each other and lower the chance of answers being given to please the interviewer.
- They give more chances for the interviewer to make sure respondents understand the questions being asked.
- The lack of any formal questionnaire lets the interviewer pursue the unexpected. (For example if a father says 'It is important for young children to be taught about AIDS because times have now changed' the interviewer can probe this answer further by asking 'Can you say more about what has changed?')

Group interviews have the disadvantages that:
- They do not always allow everyone to say freely what they think.
- One or two people may dominate the group and make it difficult for the interviewer to give everyone a chance to speak.
- The chances of introducing bias (prejudice towards views, which do not give the true situation) are high because respondents may want to please each other.

One type of group interview that has become very popular is a *focus group*. It is conducted with a specially chosen sample of respondents who share the same characteristics and experience of the topic, which is being discussed. For example, if the discussion is about mothers' views on the local antenatal clinic, then the focus group would have mothers who have just given birth. If the discussion is about the problems men have when they are unemployed then the focus group would have men who had no jobs.

Guidelines for observing an interview

1 How is rapport established?
2 Who talks most?
3 Who talks least?
4 Who gets listened to?
5 What happens if people disagree?
6 Are new or conflicting ideas expressed?
7 What does the body language and voice tone tell you?
8 How does the situation in which the interview is being conducted affect the interview?
9 How many people in the group participate? (Men, women, children.)

From experience:

Group interviews

In Sialkot, Pakistan, the local hospital became very worried about the number of patients who did not continue taking their medicine for tuberculosis (TB). To find out the reason why this was happening the hospital did a study using focus groups. Local people were trained to facilitate the focus groups. Three focus groups for men and three for women were run by a facilitator of the same sex. The respondents were all TB patients. The discussions showed that people felt they would be treated as social outcasts if their neighbours knew they had TB. They also showed that the lack of free treatment and costs of treatment (including the cost of transport to reach the hospital) caused many people to stop taking the medicine. Support from family members helped people continue the medicine. The respondents provided this sensitive information because the focus groups provided an atmosphere that was accepting and supportive. Many respondents expressed a feeling of relief after the discussion because they had been able to share their worries about their disease and the medicine. They were also able to discuss the difficulties they had in their relationships with hospital staff.

(Adapted from Liefooghe, R., Michiels, N., Habib, S., Morgan M. B., and Muynck, A. de (1995) 'Perception and social consequences of tuberculosis: a focus group study of tuberculosis patients in Sialkot, Pakistan', *Social Science and Medicine*, Vol. 41, No. 12, pp. 1685-92, Elsevier Science Ltd.)

FIGURE 11   Focus group discussion

Training exercise

Developing interview guidelines

Purpose: To provide opportunities to develop an interview guideline and the skills needed to conduct group interviews.

Time: One and a half hours: 20 minutes preparing interview guide, opening statement and questions; 15 minutes interview time; 10 minutes feedback in small groups; 5 minutes feedback per group; 15 minutes whole group concluding discussion.

Materials: Notebooks and pens/pencils.

Steps:
1 Explain the purpose of the session. Ask the participants to work in groups of six and to choose an interviewer, a note-taker and an observer. Remind the observer what to look for.
2 Ask each group to produce their own interview guide of five questions to explore a topic that the respondents will have some knowledge about. (Good topics might be their opinion on a current event or a problem that is shared by all those participating in the training.)
3 Tell them to develop an opening statement that tells the respondents the purpose of the interview and to have opening questions to start the interview.

4 Tell them they have 15 minutes to conduct the interview and ask them to start.

5 After 15 minutes stop the interviews. Ask groups to feedback to each other in their groups by asking the interviewer to say how he or she felt about the interview and to identify his or her own strengths and weaknesses. Ask the respondents to give feedback on what the interviewer did well and on how they could improve their skills. Ask the observers to give feedback on the interactions. Each person should make notes of the main strengths and weaknesses experienced by the interviewers.

6 Lead a general discussion with the whole group about the experience.

2.4   Making observations

Interviews generate information about people's ideas, attitudes and beliefs and what they say about their behaviours. Observations give us information about what people do rather than what they say they do. Direct observations allow us to see actual behaviours. They can provide more direct information than other methods. They also allow us to see the situation in which the behaviour takes place and thereby understand it better.

Observations can be a good source of information as long as they are systematic. Observations are subjective because what we see (or do not see) is influenced by our own culture and experience. For this reason we need to be clear about what we want to find out and how we will collect and record the information.

We can observe people's actual behaviour or signs of their behaviour. For example, while it is easy to observe with permission what people actually eat, it is more difficult to observe whether they use a latrine or not. We might need to look at the latrines to see evidence of use. They might be being used for other things such as storing grain. (This was the situation when a donor agency built new latrines for communities on the Zambia-Mozambique border.)

We can make observations in an obvious and interactive way by telling people what we are doing and what we are looking for, and participating in discussion with them. We may also want to make unobtrusive (hidden) observations. However, this poses the ethical problem of whether we should observe people without them knowing it.

The three main types of observations are:

• *Participant observation* where those involved from outside the community work together with local people in planning activities and at the same time observe what is going on. Participant observation helps the observer to understand the activities from the viewpoint of the local people. This type of observation is unstructured and is used to add to the information generated from interviews and written documents. The observations help to provide a better understanding of people's behaviours. For example, in the Child-to-Child 'Little Teacher' programme in Botswana, observations were made during visits to children's homes which helped planners understand how children were able to pass health messages to their parents. These observations confirmed the information gained through interviews.

- *Unstructured observation* where the observer is an on-looker, not a participant in activities. While local people know they are being observed they do not know exactly what is being observed. As with participant observations the purpose is to view behaviour in a holistic way in order to gain a fuller description of the community. These two types of observations are particularly useful in helping us understand behaviours in relation to people's physical and social situations. For example, if a planner is trying to understand the causes of malnutrition, he or she may stay for some days in the community to see what people eat.

- *Structured observations* look at small numbers of people in order to generate information for specific aspects of programme planning. The observer usually makes a list of what he or she wants to observe before starting the observation. The information generated is usually quantitative and provides little description of the situation. For example, an observer may sit in a classroom recording each time a child asks or answers a question during the lesson. In a group interview the observer may record the number of times each group member speaks. This record can help to recognise bias caused by one or two people dominating the discussions and not letting other people talk.

Below is an example of how observations helped planners and local people design an improved water supply system.

From experience:

A water supply programme in Ethiopia

In Ethiopia, a twelve-town water supply and sanitation study was carried out to make sure that each town had enough water which people could afford to buy. If this could not be done the engineers feared people would go back to their old habits of using dirty water, and water from places which were far away. The planners did a study which involved finding out the concerns of local people. They also observed health behaviours and practices concerning the use of water and hygiene. The resulting project was designed to give the right amounts of water at each location to make sure that there was a continuous supply to homes and yards as well as public fountains.

(Adapted from Almedom, A., Blumenthal, U., and Manderson, L., (1997) *Hygiene Evaluation Procedures*, ODA, INFDC, London School of Hygiene and Tropical Medicine and UNICEF.)

Training exercise

Purpose: To practise making observations.

Time: At a time when people come together to have a meal.

Materials: Paper and pens.

Steps:

1 Ask the participants to work in groups of three or four people. Their task is to make observations to find the answer to the question: Do men eat more than women? Discuss with the group the possible ethical problems of observing people without getting their consent.
2 Tell participants to make these observations whilst they are having a meal together with other people in a communal eating area. (For example they could eat lunch in a cafeteria, a communal dining hall or a restaurant.)
3 Remind them to observe the meals that other people are eating and to remember the types of food and the amounts of each food these people are eating.
4 Tell them to write down their observations as soon as they have finished their meal and left the eating area. *Tell them to record only what they saw NOT what they think the observation suggests.*
5 Ask people to discuss and compare their observations with the other members of their group, and then interpret their findings to answer the question.

2.5   Reviewing documents

The third method often used for generating qualitative information is to look at available documents. Documents can be looked at by both planners and local people. Local people can bring useful documents for review. The purpose of reading and discussing documents is to cross-check information gathered from other sources.

There are two types of documents. The first type are published and sometimes called 'black and white' literature. The second type are unpublished and known as 'grey' literature. Both types of documents are equally useful for planning. We need to search very carefully to find all the documents which are useful to us. In this way we can discover extra information which has not been generated from interviews and observations. We can also use information from documents to cross-check the information generated using other methods.

It is getting easier for us to find published documents. The Internet helps us find books and articles in publications throughout the world. Also, photocopiers allow us to get copies of articles even if we do not have access to the entire journal. Similarly we can get chapters of books without acquiring the entire book.

Grey literature is more difficult to find. However, the Internet is also making it easier to access to this type of literature. To find grey literature we need to be very committed to searching it out and to be continually on the lookout for what might be useful. We need to learn how to find out which documents are likely to be useful to us. The following are examples of grey literature:

- Government documents,
- NGO annual reports,
- Consultant reports,
- University research reports,
- Records from government offices including surveys,
- Studies undertaken by international agencies,
- Internet Web sites.

FIGURE 12   Using documents

Once we have the documents, we need time to look through them and find what is relevant for planning. Most documents have far more information than we can use. We need to know how documents are laid out and learn where to find the information we want. Although much of what we read will not be useful to us, some of the information may be just what we want and save us much time and trouble. This is illustrated in the example.

From experience:

Needs assessment in Tanzania

In Tanga, Tanzania, the municipal council decided to develop a programme to improve the health conditions of poor people living in the urban areas. In trying to identify the problems of these low-income communities, the planners decided to conduct a rapid appraisal. As part of this appraisal the council needed to find out the areas where most of the poor people lived and where there was likely to be overcrowding. Fortunately, a town plan had been commissioned three years earlier, and this plan provided good sources of information about the number of people living in different areas and where the municipal services could be found and the types of housing. Using this information the council was able to decide where it should put its efforts.

Training exercise:

Using documents

Purpose: To identify sources of information which can be useful for a needs assessment

Time: Two hours.

Materials: A range of unpublished documents gathered from local government, NGOs and community organisations.

Steps:
1 Display the documents that have been gathered together on a table.
2 Divide participants into small groups and give each group a task such as *'What problems do poor people in the area have in generating income? What are the main causes of poor health? What community activities have been undertaken to help them and what have been the results of these activities?'* The information needed to do each of the tasks must be in the documents you have displayed.
3 When the tasks are finished ask each group to show the documents from which they got the information. Ask them to say what information they found in each document.
4 Lead a discussion to help the groups share the results of their group work with each other.

2.6 Using visualisations

Having looked at the three main methods for generating qualitative information – conducting interviews, making observations and reviewing documents – we will now move on to consider how we can build up an atmosphere which helps everyone to participate. This is important, because to generate information in a way that uses participation to lead to empowerment, everyone needs to contribute. However, in situations such as meetings, the most powerful people often take control and dominate the discussions. (These people are often the professionals, the local elders or authorities.) To help avoid this happening and to build a more participatory learning atmosphere we can use a technique which involves visualisations (drawing and/or writing). Instead of inviting participants to talk about local problems we can ask each of them to write down key words or draw pictures to describe the problem. Similarly, the participants can write down possible solutions to these problems or draw pictures. (Below we describe different ways of using visualisations.)

Generating this sort of visual information not only helps people to think creatively, it also helps to promote a good atmosphere for participatory planning. This is because:

- It allows all those who are participating in generating information to give their own ideas without the need for anyone to record and interpret the information for them. By generating and displaying information in a visual form the whole group can discuss the information and reach agreement about it.
- It allows each of the people who are intended to benefit from the programme to express their own knowledge about a situation. 'Outsiders', planners and professionals can learn a great deal from this.
- It generates a great deal of information in a short time and in a way that everybody can share. It is also easy to understand the different parts of a problem from looking at the visual information.
- It provides a chance for those involved in exchanging information to gain new understanding of a situation. Even if they know the situation very well, the visual information can provide ways of looking at it in a new light and of finding new solutions to what appeared to be an unsolvable problem.

VIPP (Visualisation in Participatory Programmes)

VIPP is a way in which information can be visualised, by people writing down two or three words on cards and then displaying the cards for everyone to see and discuss. We can use VIPP to help people who are shy to get actively involved in the planning process. We can also use it to help planners and local people make joint decisions about how projects should be planned and carried out.

VIPP emerged from the experience of planning in adult education and draws on the ideas of Paolo Freire, described in Chapter 1. It has also had support from the Metaplan techniques developed in Germany. These techniques have been promoted through aid programmes run by the German government and NGOs and through their planning processes known as 'Goal (Zeil in German) Oriented Project Planning' (ZOPP).

To use VIPP to help solve a problem, for example, each participant is given thick pens and pieces of paper or cards. Each participant is invited to share his or her views on solving the problem by writing a few words in large letters on a card. A person, who is not connected with the project in any way, acts as a facilitator to guide the process. He or she collects the cards and then presents each card to the entire meeting. The facilitator helps the group to interpret the issue being discussed by grouping the cards and giving each group a large heading. The participants tell the facilitator which group to put each card into. In this way the individual cards are used to help understand the problem better and reach an agreed solution to that problem.

The value of the cards is that they allow everyone to participate in generating and interpreting the information because it takes place visually in front of the whole group. Finding and agreeing the solution is also made easier, because the discussion is supported by the words on the cards and each participant can see how this agreement was reached. People feel more able to participate because nobody needs to be identified with the card he/she wrote

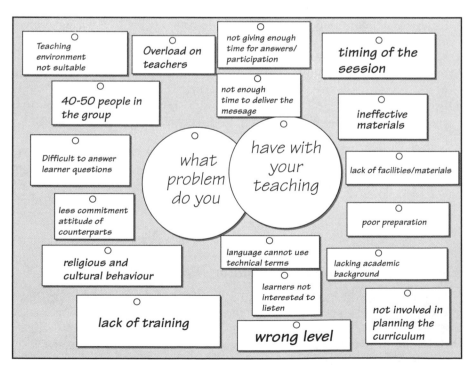

FIGURE 13   Using the VIPP approach

and this lowers the fear of other participants saying something unpleasant. Everyone is helped to participate on a more equal basis because each person can contribute by writing on a card rather having to be able to speak fluently in front of the group.

From experience:

Using VIPP in Bangladesh

In Bangladesh the Ministry of Social Welfare was responsible for co-ordinating other ministries to develop programmes for the 'Decade of the Girl Child'. It invited representatives to a workshop. The workshop began in the traditional way with a speech from the Secretary of the Ministry and a presentation on problems of the girl child. However, the facilitators then used VIPP to develop participation. They asked each participant to write down on cards the major problems facing the girl child. The cards were collected in and sorted into three groups of problems: i) education, ii) health and nutrition and iii) legal and religious matters. Participants then divided into three groups and each group was asked to discuss one of the categories of problems and then to present a role-play to the whole group to give the result of the group discussion.

Training exercise

VIPP

Purpose: To provide an opportunity for participants to use VIPP.

Time: 90 minutes.

Materials: Paper cut into pieces of 8 in × 12 in. You will need about 100 pieces depending on the size of the group. Thick pens of different colours; flipchart paper on which to place the cards; adhesive of some type which is not permanent – drawing pins or sticky gum (gum adhesive).

Steps:
1 Divide the whole group into small groups of six to eight people and give each group some small pieces of paper or card and thick pens.

2 Explain that the purpose of this exercise is to agree some rules for how we are going to work together in groups for training and planning.
3 Give examples of possible rules such as: being on time; choosing a chairperson and a recorder and rotating these roles at different meetings; listening and respecting others' views.
4 Ask the group to discuss and agree some rules and then to use the cards to write down one rule on each card.
5 Collect in all the cards and sort them into categories such as time keeping, respect, listening, etc. Stick the cards onto the flipchart sheets and display.
6 Stress that these rules are now the ground rules for working in that group. They have been agreed upon by the group rather than being imposed upon them and are the basis of the group's relationships.
7 Keep these rules visible during the training as a reminder.

VIPP is designed to promote empowerment. It can help people to participate who have previously been left out of discussions. There are problems, however, in using VIPP. For example, only people who have some skill in reading and writing can fully participate in this process. The poorest and most marginalised may have very few of these skills. It has also been reported that professionals in groups using the VIPP process can dominate local people even though using VIPP is supposed to help prevent such domination. For example, when an outside donor has already given the funds for a programme, professionals may use their power to gain agreement on issues that reflect the donor's needs and not those of the intended beneficiaries.

Using pictures

Bob Linney in his book, *Pictures, People and Power* (See Further reading in Appendix 1) shows how the use of pictures can lead to participation and empowerment. He says that pictures can help people escape from what Paolo Freire calls 'the culture of silence' and help them to 'find their own voice'. This is not a voice that can speak only in words of one syllable, but one which speaks in the rich, complex and creative language of pictures.

To lead to this situation of participation and empowerment, we need to follow three rules:

1 Start at the point where the learners (local people) are. Explore topics and issues that local people are already familiar with so that they can put forward their own ideas and thoughts. See that the value of their contribution is recognised by all those involved in generating information.
2 Ask questions and pose problems. Do not lecture people about what you think they ought to know. Ask questions to help learn about their ideas on

a topic and to understand their views and concerns.

3 Encourage active participation of all those involved. In this way a two-way learning process is created so that new knowledge is shared and not only held by the professionals.

Drawing on the methodology developed by Paulo Freire, (which we have described in Chapter 1) Linney presents guidelines for using pictures to generate information and develop shared learning (see below). This is adapted into a training exercise to show how a picture of a familiar situation can be used as the starting point for local people to identify problems and solutions and develop a plan of action.

Guidelines for discussions using pictures for empowerment and participation

1 *Describe* – encourage participants to describe what they see in the picture.
2 *Relate* – relate what is shown in the picture to their own lives.
3 *Identify the problems* – make sure that everyone in the group is clear about what are the main problems shown in the picture.
4 *Look for causes* – ask participants to look for the causes of the problem making a detailed interpretation (this is a critical stage for building awareness).
5 *Look for solutions* – encourage participants to suggest solutions, which link up with the causes they found.
6 *Plan of action* – invite the groups to make a plan of action with the aim of putting their solutions into practice.

(Adapted from Linney, B. (1995) *Pictures, People and Power*, London: Macmillans.)

Training exercise:

Using pictures

Purpose: To provide experience of using pictures to lead discussions about problems, find solutions and develop plans of action.

Time: One and a half hours.

Materials: A picture representing a problem that is familiar to all participants, flipchart papers, thick pens. (For example, the picture might show a school compound with no latrine and a child defecating on the ground behind the classroom.)

Steps:
1 Ask participants 'What can you see happening in the picture?'
2 Ask 'What problems can you see in the picture?'
3 List the problems on the flipchart using a thick pen.
4 Ask 'What solutions can we find to these problems?'
5 Write the solutions on the flipchart – next to the problem they address.
6 Together make a plan of action to solve these problems. To do this: identify problems which are important and which can easily be solved; write out what steps need to be taken to solve the problem; assign responsibilities for undertaking the steps.

2.7   Keeping information in a logbook

The information that we collect must be written down so we can use it for planning. A logbook is a small notebook in which we write down this information. We can then look back and see what we have learned so far in the planning process. The information we write down includes:

- plans for getting the information,
- information generated through interviews and observations,
- our insights and tentative conclusions,
- our own views and feelings about the process of generating information.

The logbook is the record of the information that will later be sorted out and interpreted. It is a record of the way in which our plans and ideas develop in relation to new ideas and new discoveries.

We need to start making the logbook when we first begin to seek information about a specific situation. All related information should be recorded here. Experience suggests that when collecting the information it is useful to divide the page into two columns. On the left we can record the 'descriptive' information generated through interviews and observations. On the right we can start to interpret the information. For example, after an interview, we can look back over the information we have recorded and identify major categories of response in the column on the right. For example, if people are discussing the reasons for not using the health services, major categories of response might include: 1) lack of money, 2) no drugs available at the centre, 3) poor attitude of staff. Identifying the major categories of response in this way is known as *coding* the information. This approach will start us on the process of interpreting the information. We will discuss interpreting and coding the information again later in the chapter.

In the right column of the logbook we can record information that either agrees or disagrees with information we have collected in interviews. For example, if a respondent tells us that childhood malnutrition is a problem but we do not observe any malnourished children in our work in the area, we should write this down and mark it for further checking.

From experience:

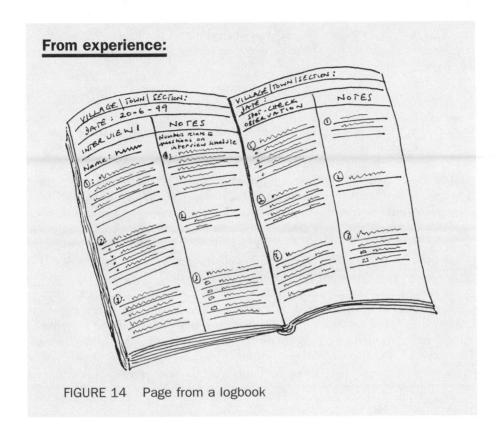

FIGURE 14   Page from a logbook

When recording information we must always distinguish between descriptions (of what people tell us and what we observe) and the interpretation or meaning we give to these descriptions. For example, we may observe that most children do not wear shoes and interpret this to mean their families are poor. We need to separate our interpretation from the information generated. We can do this by writing interpretations down in a different coloured pen or putting them in brackets.

Whatever method we use for recording information in the logbook it must always be systematic. This means that we must always place the information under the heading so it can easily be identified as 'descriptive' information or 'interpreted' information.

Having considered methods of generating and analysing information we will now move on to look at how the planning team, consisting of both professionals and beneficiaries, can check the information for accuracy by cross-checking.

2.8 Cross-checking information

By cross-checking we mean comparing information on the same issue that has been generated in different ways, for example, by interviews and observation, in order to see if it is the same. Cross-checking, or triangulation as it is often called, is important because it helps us to find out about (and overcome) any bias or error in the way we have collected or interpreted the information. Bias can happen when:

- The team talks with people who are likely to share the same attitudes and beliefs as they do. They do not talk to people who might not share these ideas. For example, they talk to government officials, not to those who are not satisfied with government services.
- The team exchanges information with people who tell them what they want to hear not what they really think or feel. They do this because they want to please the team members and make them feel good. Or they do this because they believe they may gain profit and money if they identify problems which the team can easily solve. For example, people might say they have a water problem if they know the team have money to spend to improve water supplies. Or they may tell the team they need a hospital if they know they are from the Department of Health.
- The team exchanges information, but because of their experience, background or beliefs they do not hear what is being said. They only hear what they want to hear. If they are from the health department they might hear only problems related to disease, even though other problems are mentioned. Or they might ask leading questions to get the answers they want. For example they may ask 'Don't you think that your children need to eat green vegetables every day?'

By cross-checking the information generated the planning team can help to avoid bias. There are several ways that the team can triangulate and cross-check the information.

- They can make sure they exchange information with a number of different kinds of people, including those who have different views about the questions being asked. They can make sure they have talked to people who are poor, those who are managing all right, and those who are wealthy. They can make sure they have talked to people who will be affected by their programme but traditionally are never consulted. They need to talk to women as well as men, to young people as well as old people.
- They can make sure that they use different methods to generate and interpret information. For example, they can use a mix of qualitative and quantitative methods or different techniques. (Techniques will be described in the next two chapters.)
- They can make sure that the planning teams include people of different

FIGURE 15   Talking to people of all ages

backgrounds and experiences. This will help them to make sure that they do not seek and interpret information that fits in with a narrow set of views and interests.

• They can ask other people working with the team to review their records and interpret them to see if their views agree with those of the team.

2.9   Interpreting information

Interpretation and validation of information is the key to successfully planning the programme. This must be done carefully and thoroughly and *involve the people intended to benefit from the programme at all stages of the planning process*. Information, which is not systematically and carefully interpreted and validated, is of no use to anyone.

After information has been collected and cross-checked it is necessary to bring all the information together and go through it again. The team can then decide which information is most important and develop a plan of action. To interpret qualitative information the team can follow these steps:

1 Describe the people who generated the information: 'Who were they? Why were they chosen?

2 Select the most important information and place related information under the same category or code. (This is known as *coding the information* and is described in more detail later in the chapter.)

3 Write up this summary on a flipchart to make interpretation easy. For example, draw a matrix that shows which people gave what reasons. On the following page is an example that records why people don't use the health service.

From experience:

Matrix for information about health service utilisation

Key informant/reason for not using health service	Too expensive	Too far away	Health staff unfriendly
Mothers with children under 5 years old		X	X
Male youth	X		X
Female youth			X
Adult males		X	X

4 Draw conclusions from the information in the matrix. For example, the matrix above shows that all categories of informants identify staff attitudes as a problem while mothers and adult males identify the distance they have to travel to reach a health facility as a major barrier.
5 Develop a plan for validating the findings to prove they represent the true picture of people's views. For example, ask local people to confirm these views with people they know. Ask the health staff to review the findings. Check if any documents report similar studies.

One of the most difficult steps is identifying categories of response, known as coding the information. Below are guidelines to help you in this task.

Guidelines for coding information

1 Get a sense of the whole. Read through interviews carefully. Put down ideas, which come to you as you read.
2 Pick up a record of one interview – the most interesting, the shortest, the one at the top of the pile. Go through it and ask yourself: What is the topic being discussed? What are the different sorts (categories) of ideas people have about this topic? Write down your ideas in the margins of the paper.
3 When you have gone through several interviews, list all the categories you have found. Put these into columns, which can be headed 'major categories mentioned by many people' and 'unique topics mentioned by only one or two people'. You may also have a third column with 'leftovers' that do not appear to fit in any category.
4 Now go back to your interviews. Make abbreviations for your categories, which are codes, and write these codes next to the related text.

5 Look for ways of putting your codes together by putting all related codes under one heading. You can draw lines between your codes to show they are related.
6 Finalise your codes and put them in alphabetical order so that you can find them easily if you forget what they mean.
7 Put all information related to one code under that code and do a first interpretation.
8 If this does not work well, start again and re-code your information.

(Based on Cresswell, A. (1994) *Research design qualitative and quantitative approaches*, London: Sage.)

For example, school children in London were asked 'What do some children of your age do that makes them unhealthy?' Major categories of response mentioned by many children were identified as:
1 eating unhealthy food (code uf),
2 watching too much television (code tv),
3 smoking cigarettes (code sm),
4 not washing themselves (code nw),
5 substance abuse (alcohol and illegal drugs) (code sa).
   Unique categories mentioned by only one or two children were:
1 staying up late (code ul),
2 playing computer games (code cg),
3 not doing any exercise (code ne).

After you have coded the information by deciding on the categories of response, you need to validate your findings to be sure you have interpreted the information correctly. Here are some ways this can be done.

Guidelines for validating information to be sure that you have interpreted it correctly

1 Cross-check the information again to check that it is accurate. Look for similarities and differences in information on the same issue:
   i)   from different sources (e.g. market traders and teachers),
   ii) collected by different people (e.g. male and female members of the team),
   iii) collected by different methods (e.g. interviews and observations).
2 Plan to take the information and interpretation back to the people who gave it to you and review your findings with them.
3 Decide how the people you spoke to are going to be involved further in planning, and in carrying out the plan, so that your information stays valid and accurate.

3 Choosing techniques for participation and empowerment (Part 1)

This and the next chapter describe a range of techniques to help us generate information. These techniques use one or more of the methods described in Chapter 2. The description of each technique starts by describing the technique and how it is used. Then an example is given from experience and a training exercise is presented to help develop understanding and skill in using the technique is presented. Books that give more examples can be found in the reading list given in Appendix 1, for example, the book written by Jules Pretty and his colleagues called *Participatory learning and action: a trainer's guide*.

3.1 What techniques can we use and how do we use them?

There is now a large basket of techniques available to help us generate information in a visual form. Most of these techniques fall into two types. Firstly, techniques which are used for mapping and diagramming (including charts and pictures). These will be described in this chapter. Secondly, techniques which are used for ranking and scoring. Ranking means placing items in order. Scoring means giving different values to each item according to its rank. Ranking and scoring techniques will be described in Chapter 4.

There are no blueprints for participatory development, we need to be open-minded and try out new and creative ideas. For example, during the course of a participatory appraisal several new techniques are usually developed by, and with, a community. For this reason we need to:

- *be flexible* when selecting techniques to use. We need to change techniques to fit our situation and develop new ones to fit our purpose,
- *be adaptable* so that we can fit into the physical and social situation in which the programme is to be carried out,
- *be able to generate information and interpret it 'on-the-spot'* so that local people can use the information straight away,
- *be engaged in shared learning experiences* so that these techniques stimulate discussion between local people and professionals and help develop a climate in which everyone can share their experiences in an open and transparent way. Although we have a wide range of techniques available to

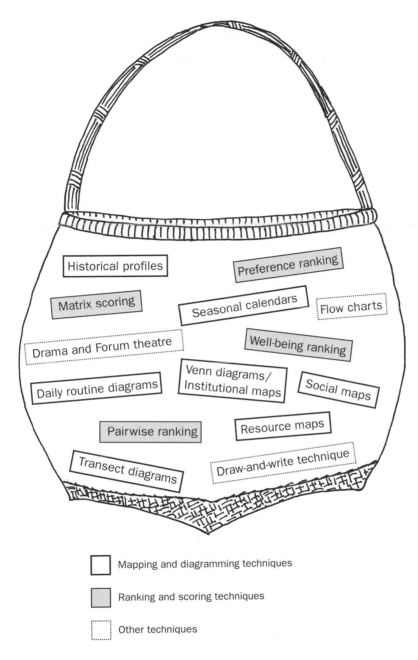

Historical profiles

Preference ranking

Matrix scoring

Seasonal calendars

Flow charts

Drama and Forum theatre

Well-being ranking

Daily routine diagrams

Venn diagrams/
Institutional maps

Social maps

Pairwise ranking

Resource maps

Transect diagrams

Draw-and-write technique

☐ Mapping and diagramming techniques

▨ Ranking and scoring techniques

⬚ Other techniques

FIGURE 16   Basket of techniques

help generate information needed we also need to have good facilitation skills in order to use these techniques. Key facilitation skills are listed on the following page.

Guidelines for being a good facilitator

- Establishing a friendly relationship at the start.
- Being supportive and energetic.
- Making everyone feel comfortable and part of the group.
- Treating people as equals. Accepting criticism and being open to learn from the group.
- Respecting everyone's ideas and the community's decisions.
- Communicating clearly and slowly – but not doing all the talking.
- Being a good listener. Listening carefully and showing that you are listening (non-verbally through facial expression).
- Being a good observer. Watching while you facilitate. Looking for signs of tiredness or boredom and responding appropriately.
- Being gender aware. Encouraging women to have more say in decision-making. Checking for understanding, energy level, or agreement. *'What did he mean?' 'How are you feeling now?'*, *'Do you agree with what she said?'*.
- Focusing the discussion around the topic chosen.
- Asking questions to find out more. *'Can you tell us more about....?'*
- Encouraging a spirit of openness and helpful questioning. Encouraging people to identify problems and work out realistic solutions.
- Showing empathy and not being judgmental, but also challenging what is said.
- Equalising participation by drawing out the silent and controlling the talkative.
- Helping to overcome disagreements.
- Praising and encouraging people. Building up individual and community self-confidence.
- Using different methods to maintain interest. For example, different sizes of groups, different activities such as discussions, pictures and drama.
- Being a good time manager. Estimating how much time each activity takes, watching the time and setting an appropriate pace for the group.
- Being flexible. Being prepared to change the programme to fit the circumstances.
- Getting the community to take responsibility for the meeting and decision-making. Reminding them it is their programme so they should make the decisions.
- Restating what has been said to make sure it has been understood correctly.
- Summarising what has been learned.
- Leaving the participants feeling motivated to meet and act on their own.

Training exercise:

Developing facilitation skills

1 Start by giving a demonstration to show the skills needed to facilitate a group discussion.
2 Choose a problem that is shared by the members of the whole group.
3 Divide the group into small groups of three or four.
4 Give each small group at least ten pieces of paper (or cards) and a thick pen. Groups can ask for more paper if they need it.
5 Encourage each person to draw one aspect of the problem on a card and to repeat this until they have run out of ideas. The drawing does not have to be 'professional' as long as the group understands what it means.
6 When people have finished drawing, bring the whole group together in a big circle. Sort the cards into different categories. Look at each card together, discuss it and decide where it should go. Ask the artists to explain what their pictures mean to the group if necessary.
7 Now lay them out to show which pictures show problems, causes of problems and effects of problems. Put the immediate causes of the problem first and then the root causes. For example, if the group is discussing teenage pregnancy, the immediate cause will be having unprotected sex, but the underlying cause may be pressure from friends to have a boyfriend and the need to find money to pay their school fees.
8 Finally ask participants 'What did you learn from this demonstration?' 'What was the purpose of the discussion?', 'What did it achieve?'
9 Now divide participants into small groups of about six people. Repeat the group discussion with the new facilitators. Give feedback in the same way.

At the start of the planning activity the facilitator divides the participants into peer groups which have members of the same sex and age. These peer groups are usually groups of older men, older women, younger men, younger women, and children. This is important because when men and women are in different groups gender analyses can be carried out. For example, gender analysis may help us to explore different workloads between men and women.

Each peer group has a facilitator, a note-taker and an observer from the planning team. (Chapter 2 looked at how to be a note-taker and an observer and there is a reminder in the box below.) Once the activity has started the facilitator will hand over their role to a local participant and support them in their role as the new facilitator. This is known as 'handing over the stick' and it is a way of sharing power within the group. When the peer groups have finished using the technique to generate information, the facilitator brings them back together to present their information to the other groups and to discuss similarities and differences.

Guidelines for taking notes: a reminder

1 Use a discreet notebook.
2 Record the detail of what is said in the exact language used. This means writing down who said what and whether others agreed.
3 Record body language and feelings expressed.
4 Record how the activity went.
5 After the interview talk with the observer and add more information to your notes.
6 Record your own personal impressions.

Guidelines for observing group interviews: a reminder

1 How is rapport established?
2 Who talks most?
3 Who talks least?
4 Who gets listened to?
5 What happens if people disagree?
6 Are new or conflicting ideas expressed?
7 What does the body language and voice tone tell you?
8 How does the situation in which the activity is taking place affect the generation of information?
9 How many people in the group participate?

3.2   Techniques for mapping and diagramming

A map or diagram is a drawing that presents information in a simple visual way that is easy to understand. Even people who have not been to school can draw diagrams to show aspects of their lives. These diagrams can help people to understand their situation and the causes of problems and find ways to solve them. Maps, diagrams and charts are usually drawn with chalk or thick pens on a board or paper or they can be drawn on the ground outside with a stick.

Some maps tell us how things relate to each other in a geographical area, others tell us how things relate to each other over time. Some commonly used maps and diagrams that have been found most useful from experience are described in this chapter. They can be summarised as:

Maps related to geographical location	Maps related to time
• Resource maps • Social maps • Venn diagrams / institutional maps • Transect diagrams	• Seasonal calendars • Historical profiles • Daily routine diagrams

3.3   Geographical maps

Community resource maps and social maps

The maps most commonly drawn by local people are community resource maps and social maps. Resource maps show natural and physical resources and the use of these resources. For example forests, vegetation, hills, mountains, agricultural land, rivers, dams, wells, fallow land, fertility of the land, cropping patterns, fertiliser use, soil type, crop yields, livestock, footpaths and boundaries. These maps also show schools, churches, health facilities, latrines and roads.

Social maps show individual households that make up the community. It can be useful to record the name of the head of each household. Symbols can be used to show different household characteristics. For example, those households which have special needs due to food insecurity, malnutrition, pregnancy or disability, or because the head of the household is a widow. Social maps may also show how many people (men, women, pre-school and school-age children) live in each household, and show where people live who are trusted as helpers in different matters (community health workers, traditional birth attendants, spiritual leaders, religious leaders, traditional

From experience:

A resource map

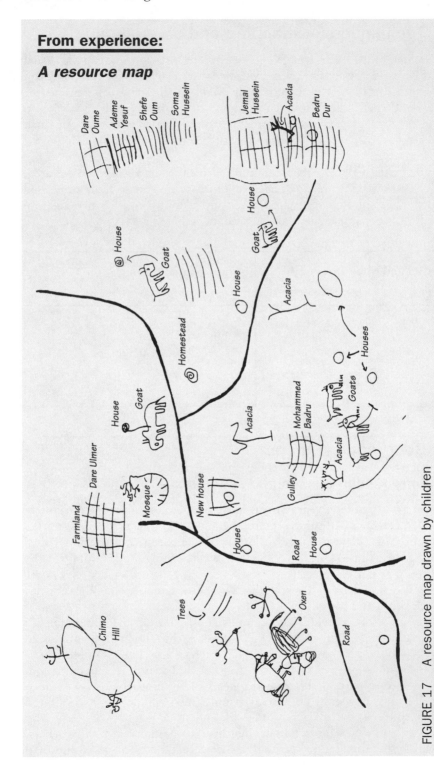

FIGURE 17   A resource map drawn by children

(*Source:* Neela Mukherjee, (1992) 'Villagers Perceptions of Rural Poverty Through the Mapping Method of PRA', *PRA Notes No. 15*, London: International Institute of Environment and Development.)

leaders, school teachers). Social maps can show where sections of the community live who share kinship ties, political or religious affiliation or who are long-time residents or newcomers or who live in greater poverty. Other areas which can be shown are those which are safe or unsafe, polluted, littered, mosquito-breeding grounds, sacred places, markets, latrines, places of entertainment, schools. When people are working in peer groups to draw maps the information from all the maps can be discussed and pooled.

From experience:

A community social map

Local people in Berapal village, West Bengal, explored their perceptions of rural poverty by drawing social maps. They started by drawing the boundaries of their village, the roads, the agricultural land and the location of each household. Next they developed their own indicators of poverty such as households headed by widows, and agricultural labourers who had no land and no regular source of income or food. Then they used these indicators to rank each household on a scale of one (poorest) to four (richest).

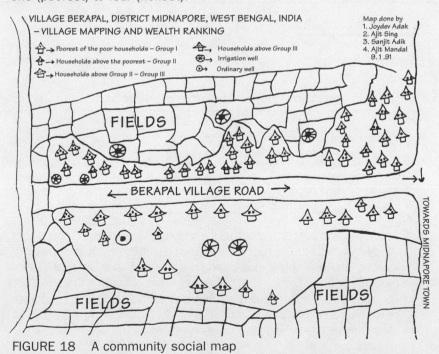

FIGURE 18   A community social map

(*Source:* Neela Mukherjee, (1992), 'Villagers' Perceptions of Rural Poverty Through the Mapping Method of PRA', *PRA Notes No. 15,* London: International Institute of Environment and Development.)

These two types of maps are often combined so that only one map is drawn showing both resources and social factors. Maps may be drawn to show resources and social factors as they were in the past. These maps can be used, for example, to generate discussion on the causes and effects of poor land use. Some people, however, prefer to draw separate resource maps and social maps because they feel that combining the maps causes confusion and makes it more difficult to manage issues arising from the map. The discussion of social maps often raises issues about where different groups live and places where people go to socialise within the community. These issues provide a chance for the facilitator to stimulate further discussion and/or introduce further techniques such as well-being ranking described later in this chapter.

Individuals rather than groups can draw personal maps. These maps show the views of different sections of the community (men and women, rich and poor, etc.) in relation to the boundaries of the community and the places that are most important to them. In the following pages we describe a number of different kinds of maps. Team members who are going to conduct the planning exercise only need to practise the techniques which they will be using with the community in the field. So many techniques are now available that it is not useful to give participants tasks that are not directly related to the fieldwork.

Training exercise:

Drawing maps

Purpose: To introduce the importance of maps and to practise mapping.

Time: Two hours.

Materials: Large copy or overhead transparencies of the community social map (FIGURE 18). Copies of any other types of community maps that you may have.

Steps:
1 Explain that maps can help the community and the planning team understand the local situation and make decisions. It can be very useful to make maps with the community at the start of a needs assessment because:
   • Local people enjoy drawing maps and have a very accurate knowledge of their surroundings.
   • Mapping gets everyone involved and used to visualising his or her knowledge.
   • Maps show what the different peer groups think is important in their community. Together with the discussion that goes on while the map is being drawn, the facilitator can quickly raise

awareness of different development issues in the community.
- Maps help to make sure that everyone can be reached and that no one is forgotten or 'invisible' within the community. They help us to plan home visits, identify different groups and sectors with different problems, foresee risky situations and find good times to hold meetings and do activities.

2 Display the example of a community map (FIGURE 18) with an explanation above it. Explain resource maps and social maps and display any other examples available.

3 Divide participants into peer groups according to age and sex and explain that they will be working with peer groups in the community. Invite each group to select a facilitator and draw a combined resource and social map of the community in which the needs assessment is going to be conducted (or another community which the group know well). Ask them to start by drawing the boundaries of the community and putting in the main roads and paths before adding other natural resources and social features. Provide any available maps or aerial photos of the area for participants to use.

4 Help each group to choose a suitable place to get started (ground, floor, paper, chalkboard). Provide thick pens if needed but otherwise let people choose the materials they want to use (such as sticks, stones or seeds) and allow them to draw the map by themselves. Be patient and do not interrupt them. It's their map!

5 Bring the groups together and walk around to visit and discuss the maps from each peer group. Encourage people to ask questions about what is shown – this is sometimes called 'interviewing the diagram'.

6 Make a list of all the ideas that have come up from the drawings and discussion and list any further questions that need to be answered.

7 Explain the roles that the facilitators, note-takers and observers from the team will play in the peer groups, when the needs assessment is conducted with the community.

Venn diagrams/institutional maps

What are they?

Venn diagrams consist of a series of circles of different sizes. The circles may be drawn so that they link together and overlap each other, or they may be drawn far apart as explained below. The circles are used to show the key institutions and people in a community. (Venn diagrams have also been called a variety of other names, such as Chapatti diagrams and Ugali diagrams, because the circles look rather like these foods.) An example of a Venn diagram is given in FIGURE 19.

How are they used?

Peer groups can draw Venn diagrams to show the relationships and links between their community or group and institutions, organisations and individuals who are involved in decisions which affect them. The diagrams show how much influence these organisations, institutions and people have on the community and how much contact the community has with them. For example, a large circle that is far from the central circle means that this organisation has great importance but little contact with the group or community.

From experience:

Venn diagram/institutional map

In 1993 a group of 17 women from Mpewa Village, in the Eastern Province of Zambia, were asked to draw a Venn diagram to show the institutions and organisations that were important to them. They drew the Venn diagram shown below on the ground using chalk.

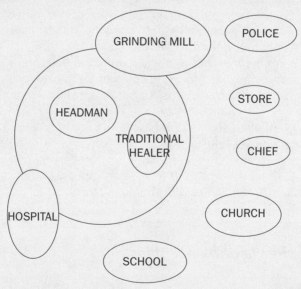

FIGURE 19   Venn diagram

The women explained their Venn diagram, saying for example:

- *The Headman* is seen as very important – he helped bring the grinding mill to the village; he settles local conflicts and mobilises the community to help the needy.

- The *traditional healer* is seen as easier to reach (drawn inside the community) than the hospital (drawn outside); the *chief* is drawn outside the community since he does not visit.
- The *church* is placed outside the community as it 'doesn't seem to be helping much anymore' though its spiritual function is still seen as important.

The women then went on to produce a Venn diagram showing the relationships as they would ideally like them to be. This vision included, for example, having the church back in the community again and having the traditional healer less important than the hospital.

(*Source:* Adapted from the World Bank (1994), *Zambia Poverty Assessment*, Report No. 12985-ZA, Vol. V: Participatory Poverty Assessment, Southern Africa Department, Human Resources Division, Washington, D.C.)

Training exercise

Venn diagrams

Purpose: To introduce and practise Venn diagrams.

Time: One and a half hours.

Materials: A large copy or overhead transparency of the Venn diagram (FIGURE 19). Paper of two different colours, glue, scissors.

Steps:
1 Explain what Venn diagrams are and why they are used. Display the example given above.
2 In small groups, ask participants to select a facilitator. Explain that they are going to make a Venn diagram to show the key institutions, organisations and people that are responsible for decisions affecting their community or group.
3 Ask participants to start by cutting out circles of different sizes from one of the coloured sheets. Then ask them to place one of these circles in the centre of a large sheet of paper of a different colour to represent their community or group. (If participants are drawing on the floor or ground they will not need to cut out paper circles.)
4 Now ask participants to choose (or draw) circles of different sizes from those they have cut out, depending on the relative importance of the individual/ institution represented. A big circle represents a very important person or organisation, a smaller circle represents a less important one.

5 Explain that if the circles are separate this means that there is no contact between the individuals/institutions. If the circles are touching then information is shared between them. If there is a small overlap there is some co-operation in decision-making and if there is a large overlap then there is considerable co-operation.

5 When the groups have finished, walk around as a whole group to view and discuss each of the diagrams. Ask questions, for example, about how things have changed in the past ten or twenty years, about what kinds of improvements they would like to see regarding the institutions and individuals represented.

6 Keep a paper record of the diagram and participants' names to give them credit.

(Adapted from Gordon, G. and Pridmore, P. (1997) *Participatory approaches to nutrition and sexual health.* DANIDA, Nairobi /Institute of Education, London.)

Transect diagrams

What are they?

Transect diagrams are a means of generating more information after social and resource maps have been drawn. They are diagrams that show the relationship of people, structures and resources in a specific area that the planners and community people have walked through together.

How are they used?

A transect diagram is prepared by a group of about six people, including members of the community, who know the area well and are willing and able to join in the walk. The group also includes outsiders/professionals, two of whom perform the roles of facilitator and note-taker. Before starting the walk, the group discusses the different things they are going to draw, and to agree the route they will need to take so that they will be able to see these things.

The group then walks along the agreed route. As they walk, the facilitator encourages them to look out for signs of problems and opportunities which have been identified in earlier exercises such as drawing the community map. The note-taker keeps a written record in a field diary of the discussion and makes notes from which to draw up the transect later. The team members need to be very observant on the walk and may go away from the original route if something of special interest is seen. The group may also visit homesteads and talk with people they meet along the way to help them learn more about important issues. Before leaving the community the note-taker draws the transect showing the main features. The aim is to give a general idea of the area rather than trying to be too accurate. The transect diagram is then shown to the other members of the group to cross-check the accuracy of the information. The transect is revised throughout the field work as learning increases.

From experience:

Transect diagrams

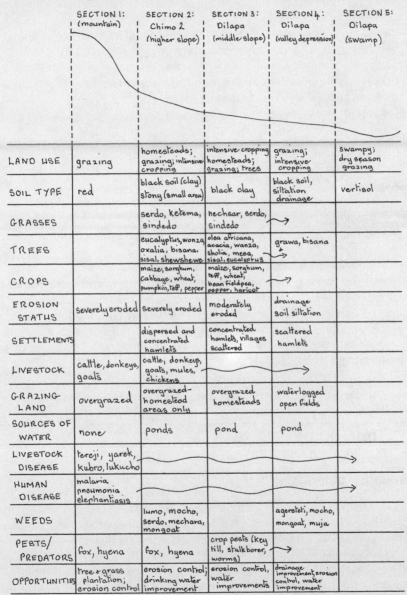

	SECTION 1: (mountain)	SECTION 2: Chimo 2 (higher slope)	SECTION 3: Dilapa (middle slope)	SECTION 4: Dilapa (valley depression)	SECTION 5: Oilapa (swamp)
LAND USE	grazing	homesteads; grazing; intensive cropping	intensive cropping homesteads; grazing; trees	grazing; intensive cropping	swampy; dry season grazing
SOIL TYPE	red	black soil (clay) stony (small area)	black clay	black soil, siltation drainage	vertisol
GRASSES		serdo, ketema, sindedo	nechsar, serdo, sindedo	→	
TREES		eucalyptus, wonza oxalia, bisana, sisal, shewshewe	olea africana, acacia, wanza, sholia, mesa, sisal, eucalyptus	grawa, bisana →	
CROPS		maize, sorghum, cabbage, wheat, pumpkin, teff, pepper	maize, sorghum, teff, wheat, bean fieldpea, pepper, haricot	→	
EROSION STATUS	severely eroded	severely eroded	moderately eroded	drainage soil siltation	
SETTLEMENTS		dispersed and concentrated hamlets	concentrated hamlets, villages scattered	scattered hamlets	
LIVESTOCK	cattle, donkeys, goats	cattle, donkeys, goats, mules, chickens		→	
GRAZING LAND	overgrazed	overgrazed- homestead areas only	overgrazed homesteads	waterlogged open fields	
SOURCES OF WATER	none	ponds	pond	pond	
LIVESTOCK DISEASE	tereji, yarek, kubro, lukucho				→
HUMAN DISEASE	malaria pneumonia elephantiasis				→
WEEDS		lumo, mocho, serdo, mechara, mongoat		agereteti, mocho, mongoat, muja	
PESTS/ PREDATORS	fox, hyena	fox, hyena	crop pests (key till, stalkborer, worms)	→	
OPPORTUNITIES	tree + grass plantation; erosion control	erosion control; drinking water improvement	erosion control, water improvements	drainage improvement, erosion control, water improvement	

FIGURE 20   Transect diagram

(*Source:* IIED (1992) 'Look who's talking: a report of a training of trainers course in participatory rural appraisal in Dalocha, Southerrn Shewa, Ethiopia', IIED/Action Aid, p.89.)

Training exercise:

Transect diagrams

Purpose: To introduce and practise transect diagrams.

Time: One and a half hours.

Materials: A large copy or overhead transparency of the transect diagram (FIGURE 20). Squared paper for drawing the transect (optional).

Steps:
1 Explain what transects are and how to use them.
2 Divide the group into small groups of six to eight people.
3 Ask them
    i)   to plan a short transect walk across the compound in which the training is taking place,
    ii) to select a facilitator and note-taker and walk along the transect route,
    iii) to draw the transect diagram and discuss it.
4 Invite the whole group to go around to view and discuss the diagrams.
5 Lead a discussion about what people have learned from the exercise.
If the compound where the training is being held is not good for practising this technique then ask the groups to draw a transect of a community they know well.

3.4   Time maps

Seasonality calendars

What are they?

Seasonality calendars are diagrams drawn by local people showing the main activities, problems and opportunities in a community throughout the year. They show factors that are important in people's lives and the months when community activities should be planned so as not to come at the busiest times of year. They can help to identify the months when different people are most at risk of, for example, food shortages or malaria, and when mothers are most stressed and unable to look after their children well. They can also help us to carry out gender analyses to understand the different tasks and workloads of men and women.

How are they used?

Seasonality calendars drawn by peer groups can give very useful information about seasonal trends within their community. These trends need only be shown in approximate numbers (there is no need for accurate measures of, for example, acreage of crops, or person-hours of labour). The group discussion, which goes on as the diagram is being drawn, is a very important means of cross-checking the accuracy of the information being generated. Seasonality calendars can give information on a wide variety of issues including:
- seasons, climate (rainfall and temperature),
- sequence of cropping (planting, weeding, harvesting, marketing),
- collection of wild fruits and herbs,
- price changes of foodstuffs,
- amount and type of food eaten,
- cycles of hunger and malnutrition, number of meals per day,
- availability of fuel,
- livestock cycles of birth, weaning, sales, migration, fodder,
- crop and livestock pests and diseases,
- income generating activities,
- availability of paid employment,
- income, expenditure and debt,
- labour demand for men, women and children,
- migration of people out of the community,
- presence of human diseases including malaria, diarrhoea and sexually transmitted diseases,
- well-being of small children,
- cycles of fertility, childbirth and breastfeeding,
- sexual activity,
- leisure, social events and festivals such as marriages, and puberty rites.

When peer groups are drawing seasonal calendars they will have a facilitator, a note-taker and observer from the planning team with them. As mentioned earlier in this chapter, the facilitator will quickly 'hand over the stick' to local participants and provide support to them in their role. The calendar usually covers a period of one calendar year but participants do not need to start it in January unless they want to. They do not need to use a Western calendar if they have a local or feast-day calendar. (Non-monthly intervals may be used.)

From experience:

Seasonality calendars

Health problems	J	F	M	A	M	J	J	A	S	O	N	D
Malaria	4	2	1							8	7	6
Cough					6	3	4	9				
STD						9	9					
TB	1	1	1	1	1	1	1	1	1	1	1	1
High blood pressure										5	3	
Wounds	5											5
Burns						8	6					
AIDS	1	1	1	1	1	1	1	1	1	1	1	1
Headache	1	1	1	1	1	1	1	1	1	1	1	1
Madness	8	3	4	4	3	3	1	1	1	1	1	8
Pregnancy	3	2	1	7	2	2	1	7	1	2	2	7

FIGURE 21   A seasonality calendar of health problems

(Source: Shah, M., Kambou, S. and Monahan, B. (1999) *Embracing Participation in Development*, Atlanta: CARE.)

This calendar was drawn by a group of girls in South Chilenje Compound, Lusaka. This group used the 12 month calendar to analyse variations over a year.

Numbers in the cells indicate the relative score (using free scoring method) for prevalence of a health problem during different months in a year. The higher the score the higher the intensity of prevalence during that month. This group analysed that AIDS, headache and TB have no seasonal pattern and are prevalent throughout the year. That's why they gave a score of 1 for all the months. There is high incidence of STDs and burns during June and July – the cold season.

Pregnancy was added to the list, even though it was mentioned that it is not exactly a health problem, but it is related to health and has a seasonal pattern.

Training exercise:

Seasonality calendars

Purpose: To show how to present complicated information on a seasonality calendar.

Time: One and a half hours.

Materials: A large copy or overhead transparency of the seasonality calendar (FIGURE 21) and any others you might have. Flipchart and paper if needed.

Steps:
1 Explain what seasonality calendars are and how they are used.
2 Divide into groups of men and women, each with a facilitator, note-taker and observer, as would happen in the community. Remind the groups that the facilitator's role is to get everyone involved in putting the symbols on the calendar, the note-taker keeps a record of the discussion, and the observer keeps a record of who participates and who does not.
3 Ask the groups to draw a seasonality calendar for a community, which at least one member of the group knows well, using symbols and not words. If the group is working on the ground they need to start by finding some handy objects such as stones and leaves that can be used as symbols. They will need a pile of each. If they are working on paper they can draw symbols.
4 If they are using a Western calendar, suggest that they start by marking months along the top of the diagram to show the months of the year and then use beans, stones, etc. to mark those that belong to the rainy, dry and cold seasons.
5 Explain that the next step is for them to choose symbols (or draw pictures) to represent work activities (such as planting, sowing, weeding) and put them in the correct months on their calendar. They can use different numbers of the chosen symbols (such as sticks or stones) to indicate the workload for each activity in a particular month.
6 After this they are ready to list, down the left-hand side of the diagram, the things which are important to them, such as food supply, hunger and malnutrition, domestic violence and teenage pregnancy, and mark the times of the year when these problems are most likely to occur. They should discuss the reasons why this is so.
7 When each group has finished their seasonality calendar bring the whole group together and go around visiting each diagram in turn. Ask individual groups to explain their diagram and then invite the whole group to interview it. Ask people how the community and the project team can work together at different seasons to improve the situation in the community at difficult times of the year. Ask how seasonal changes in the community may affect the project's work-plan – are there times when community activities can take place?

Historical profiles

What are they?

Historical profiles, often known as time lines, are diagrams in which a line is drawn to represent a period of time, usually in decades, from as far back as people can remember up until the present. (Some groups have also drawn time lines to predict what may happen in the next ten years.) Along this line significant events which have occurred in the community are marked. Time lines may show:

- changes in the patterns of rainfall, soil fertility and cropping patterns, land tenure, food consumption, malnutrition, ways of feeding children, and diseases,
- changes in the pattern of marriage, sexual activity and ways of coping,

From experience:

Historical profiles

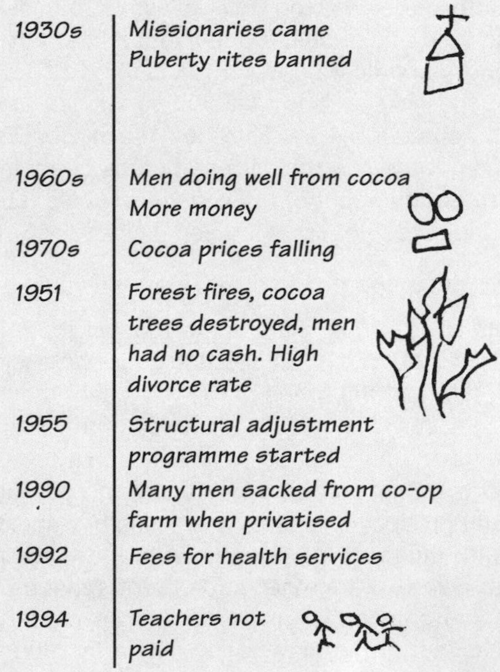

1930s	Missionaries came Puberty rites banned
1960s	Men doing well from cocoa More money
1970s	Cocoa prices falling
1951	Forest fires, cocoa trees destroyed, men had no cash. High divorce rate
1955	Structural adjustment programme started
1990	Many men sacked from co-op farm when privatised
1992	Fees for health services
1994	Teachers not paid

FIGURE 22   An historical profile in Ashanti, Ghana

- the building of infrastructure such as roads, schools, canals and railroads,
- the impact of previous projects,
- changes in administration and organisation,
- major political events.

The information that is generated by community people can be added to from historical records in books and reports.

How are they used?

By providing an overview of key historical events in the community, historical profiles can help us understand the present situation in the community, for example how drought can lead to malnutrition. Historical profiles are often carried out with elderly people who can remember the past and with community leaders and teachers. They can help people to relax together at the beginning of an interview, especially with other elderly people or with groups.

Historical profiles can be drawn on the ground using locally available materials such as sticks, stones and other objects to mark key events. It may also be helpful to draw pictures on pieces of paper which participants can move around as they remember new events. These profiles usually explore issues that have been previously identified through techniques such as drawing community maps and seasonal calendars.

Training exercise:

Historical profiles

Purpose: To introduce and practise drawing an historical profile.

Time: 40 minutes.

Materials: A large copy or overhead transparency of the historical profile (FIGURE 22). Flipchart paper and thick pens.

Steps:
1 Explain what historical profiles are and how they are used.
2 Show the example given above and any others you may have.
3 In small groups ask participants to think back in time as long as they are able to and to construct an historical profile of their own community, using the categories listed above (changes in the pattern of rainfall, marriage, roads, etc.).
4 In the classroom this drawing can be done on flipchart paper using pens, but explain that with the community it is better drawn on the ground using symbols to ensure that everyone can participate.

Daily routine diagrams

What are they?

These diagrams show the activities which people do over a period of 24 hours. They may look like a straight line with activities marked along it or they may be drawn as circular pie charts. These types of diagrams are illustrated below.

From experience:

Daily routine diagrams

The daily routine diagrams shown below have been drawn as pie charts by community members in Karnataka State, India.

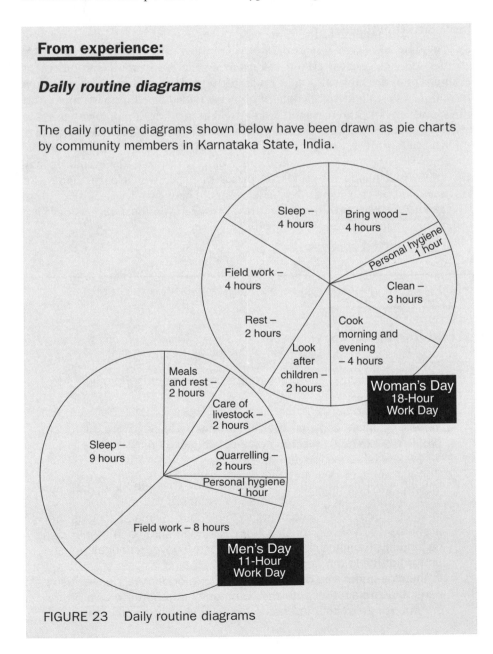

FIGURE 23   Daily routine diagrams

How are they used?

They are used to help individuals and peer groups show how they spend their time. These diagrams make it easy to carry out a gender analysis by comparing the daily activities of women and men. They can also be used to compare activities of other groups such as i) employed and unemployed, ii) married women and widows.

When the peer groups are explaining their diagrams to the whole group the facilitator can encourage the group to think of reasons for any differences between the diagrams. In the same way that seasonal calendars can show us the busiest times of the year, a daily activity chart can show the busiest times of day and can therefore be useful in helping to plan the timing of project activities. For example, they can show the best time of day for organising a training course. They can also help project workers to plan their day and do their work well. Daily routine diagrams help us to understand more about the things that affect our own well-being and social development and also that of the project and the community.

Training exercise:

Daily routine diagrams

Purpose: To introduce and practise drawing daily routine diagrams.

Time: One and a half hours.

Materials: A large copy or overhead transparency of the daily routine diagrams given above and any others you may have. Flipchart paper and pens if needed.

Steps
1 Explain what a daily routine diagram is and how it can be used. Ask people to share any experience they have of using this technique. Show the example given above and discuss it.
2 Show any other examples you may have.
3 Tell participants that they are going to draw their own daily routine diagrams – one diagram for a day in the week and one diagram for a day at the weekend.
4 Brainstorm a list of factors they may want to include, for example:

- work in the home,
- work outside the home,
- income generation inside the home,
- income generation outside the home,
- time for self and relaxation,

- time with children,
- time with partner,
- time for community activities,
- time for paid employment.

5 When people have finished drawing their own daily routine diagrams ask them to get together with participants who are of the same gender, occupation, marital status or age as themselves.
6 They can then compare their diagrams, look for common patterns and make a group diagram from the individual ones.
7 In a whole group display and discuss the group diagrams. Ask participants to think how this analysis of their daily activities relates to their own health and well-being. What benefits would there be if women did not have so much work to do?

4 | Choosing techniques for participation and empowerment (Part 2)

Having described techniques for mapping and diagramming in Chapter 3, this chapter moves on to describe techniques for ranking and scoring[1]. It also describes other commonly used techniques such as flow charts, draw-and-write, drama and Forum Theatre.

Chapter 2 explained that when professionals are working together with local people using these techniques to generate and interpret information we need to have a facilitator, a note-taker and an observer from the planning team. (See Chapters 2 and 3 for a description of the role played by each of these people). It also explained that these techniques are generally used with peer groups that have people of the same age and sex (for example, young men, old men, young women, old women, children). Each peer group has a facilitator, observer and note-taker. After using the technique the peer groups are brought back together to display their diagrams and share their learning with each other. Working in peer groups is important because it allows low status groups (often the women and children) to support each other in generating information and in sharing it with the whole group.

4.1   Techniques for ranking and scoring

We can ask key individuals or groups to rank problems or issues by putting them in their order of importance. People can use their own way of deciding how important one problem or issue is compared to another. The items (problems or issues) can then be scored, giving the highest score to the item at the top of the list and the lowest score to the item at the bottom.

It is often easier to prioritise issues in this way than to get accurate measurements of how big one problem or issue is compared to another. After people have finished ranking the items it is important to find out the reasons why they placed them in this order. We can use these techniques, together with semi-structured interviews, to generate information to help us write useful questions for more structured interviews.

Some of the most commonly used techniques are listed below:

- preference ranking,
- pairwise ranking,

83

- matrix scoring,
- well-being or wealth ranking.

We can use the first three of these techniques to help identify priority concerns. Which one is most useful depends on the situation but more than one can be used to cross-check information. Well-being or wealth ranking is used to look at distribution of well-being or wealth in a community.

Preference ranking

What is it?

This is a technique that lets us quickly find out how local people rank a set of items such as foods or problems in their community. It lets us compare the priorities or choices of different individuals or peer groups. Voting is also a form of preference ranking.

How is it used?

After a list of the main problems has been made using techniques such as community mapping and transect walks, we can use preference ranking with individuals or peer groups from the community to prioritise the problems. To do this the facilitator starts by showing the list of problems previously identified. This list is usually made up of simple pictures to represent the items rather than words. For example, if 'poor growth and development of young children in the community' is the issue then the linked problems might be:

- shortage of foods that give energy, such as oils/fats and sugar,
- children being left at home when mothers are working in the field,
- overworked mothers with little time for food preparation.

If the group is large the facilitator can then carry out a vote (by show of hands) to find out how the group ranks a set of problems. Another way of ranking the problems is to give each person a pile of stones and ask them to give one stone to the problem they think is least important, two stones to the problem they think is slightly more important and so on until they give the greatest number of stones to the problem that is most important. The problems can then be ranked according to the total number of stones each one has been given. The problem with the most stones is placed first.

With a small group of literate people, each person can write down the problems in their own order of preference, putting the most important at the top of the list. Each problem can then be scored. If there are six problems, the most important problem gets six points, the next five, the next four and so on until the problem with the lowest priority gets one. When the points are counted up for each problem they can then be ranked according to the group score. This technique is shown in the following experience.

From experience:

Preference ranking

Each participant was asked to place five problems that lowered agricultural production in their order of importance. The problem they had chosen as the most important was given a score of five, the next four, and so on. The total score from all the participants for each problem was worked out and then the problems were ranked. The result is shown in FIGURE 24.

Problem	Respondent (participant) A B C D E F	Total score	Ranking
Drought	5 5 3 5 4 5	27	a
Pests	4 3 5 4 5 4	25	b
Weeds	3 4 4 1 3 3	18	c
Costs of inputs	2 1 2 2 2 2	11	d
Labour shortage	1 2 1 3 1 1	9	e

FIGURE 24   Preference ranking

5 = most important, 1 = least important

(*Source:* Adapted from Theis and Grady (1991) 'Participatory Rapid Appraisal for Community Development', London: IIED/SCF, p. 64.)

Training exercise:

Preference ranking

Purpose: To introduce and practise preference ranking.

Time: One and a half hours.

Materials: A large copy or overhead transparency of the example of preference ranking shown above and any others you may have. Flipchart paper and pens if needed.

Steps:
1 Explain what preference ranking is and how it is used.
2 Show the example given above and any others you may have, and explain each of them.

3 Divide participants into small groups and explain that they are going to practise ranking and scoring the food that they prefer to eat.
4 Ask each group to:
  i)   agree a list of six meals that they like to eat (for example rice and beans),
  ii) write down individually their preference ranking for these six meals and score each meal giving six points to the one they like best, five to the next and so on. The group may choose to use pictures to represent each meal rather than words,
  iii) add up the total scores given to each meal and then rank the meals in order of group preference.
5 Discuss the results.

Pairwise ranking

What is it?

This is another technique that helps us find out the main preferences or priorities of individuals or groups for a set of items. It also lets us compare the priorities of different individuals.

How is it used?

The participants start by agreeing a list of about six items to be ranked and write them down or choose handy objects such as sticks, stones, leaves or flowers to represent each item. Then they draw a large square using a thick pen on a flipchart or chalk on a board or a stick on the ground outside. They place the written items, or the objects representing these items, to be scored across the top of the square and also down the left-hand side of the square. Lines are then drawn to turn the square into a matrix or grid as shown in the example given opposite.

Starting with the top right-hand square the participants compare the two different items and decide which one they prefer. The written item or object being used for this item is then put into the square. They then move from square to square in a similar manner comparing the two items and recording their preference. Two items that are the same cannot be compared and so the square is left blank or a cross is placed in it.

When all the preferences have been recorded the first item is taken and the number of preferences for this item is counted up. This is done again for each of the items. The items are finally ranked in order of the group preferences.

From experience:

Pairwise ranking

The grid below shows the results of using pairwise ranking to prioritise the reasons for girls not attending school in a village in The Gambia. The grid was developed as we have described above. The participants started in the top right-hand corner and compared early marriage with lack of facilities. They agreed that lack of facilities was the more important reason and recorded their decision in the square. They then moved from square to square until they had completed the grid.

Problems	Lack of facilities	Pregnancy	School fees	Losing traditional values	Distance from home	Early marriage
Lack of facilities		lack of facilities	lack of facilities	lack of facilities	lack of facilities	lack of facilities
Pregnancy			pregnancy	pregnancy	pregnancy	pregnancy
School fees				school fees	school fees	school fees
Losing traditional values					distance from home	early marriage
Distance from home						early marriage
Early marriage						

FIGURE 25   Pairwise ranking

When they had finished filling in the grid (as shown above) they added up the number of times each reason had been recorded as the preferred choice and ranked the reasons accordingly. As shown below, lack of facilities and pregnancy were found to be the most important reasons for girls not attending school.

Problems	No. of times preferred	Rank
Lack of facilities	5	1
Pregnancy	4	2
School fees	3	3
Early marriage	2	4
Distance from home	1	5
Losing traditional values	0	6

(*Source:* Adapted from E. Kane (1995), *Groundwork: Participatory Research for Girl's Education. A Manual to be Used with Groundwork: The Video,* World Bank, Economic Development Institute, Human Resources and Poverty Division and Asia Technical Department, Human Resources and Social Development Division, Washington, D.C.)

From experience:

Matrix scoring

FIGURE 26 was drawn by young women in The Gambia to show their matrix scoring (and ranking) of vegetables.

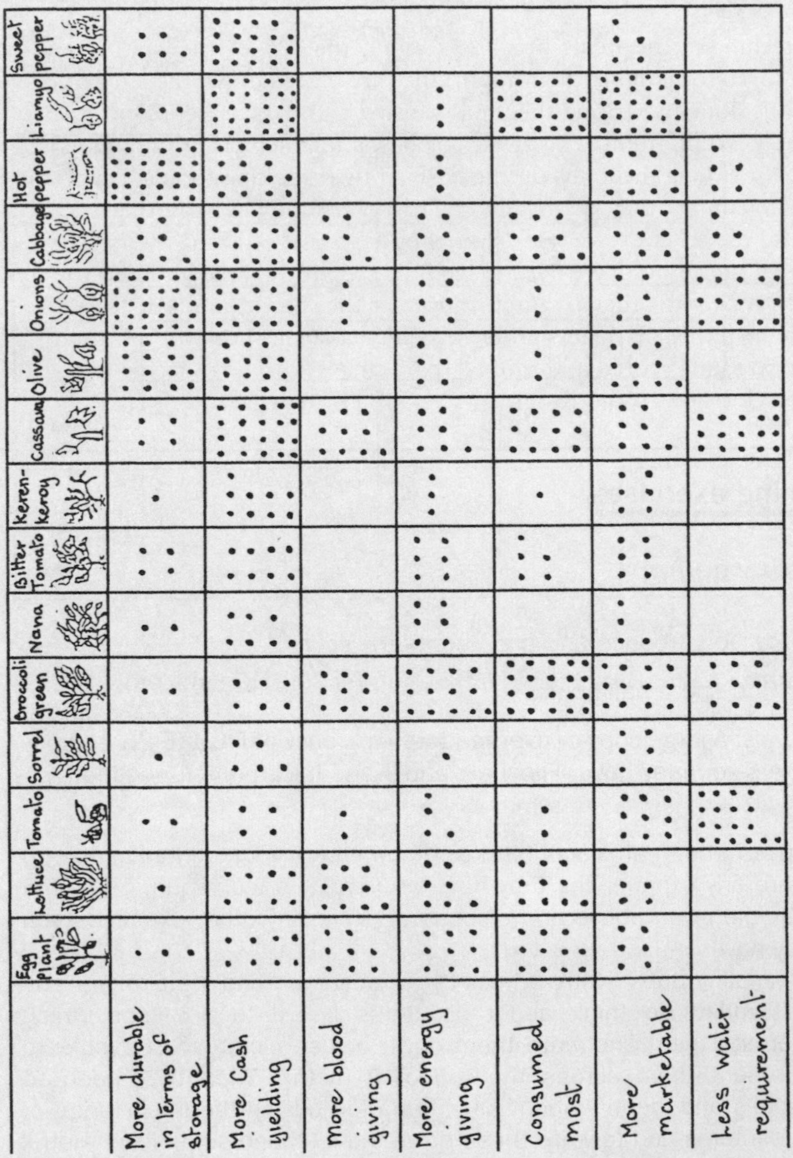

FIGURE 26   Matrix scoring

(*Source:* IIED (1992) 'Input to Impact: PRA for Action Aid, The Gambia', London: IIED.)

Matrix scoring

What is it?

A matrix is a rectangle, divided into squares, as shown in FIGURE 26 opposite, that is used to directly record the ranking that the participants give to a particular item. The item might be a vegetable (as shown in FIGURE 26), or a problem or an intervention,

How is it used?

In this technique the items are listed along the top of the matrix and the criteria (basis) for judging their importance are placed down the left-hand side. This can be done by writing the item or using an object to represent it. People are given a certain number of stones or beans for each criterion and asked to divide them among the items on the basis of their ranking for each criterion in turn. For example, they might give one stone to the criterion that they rank lowest and ten stones to the one they rank highest.

When all the stones have been placed the scores are added up and the items are then ranked in order of importance. In the final ranking factors can be weighted in terms of their significance to make the ranking more valid. If problems are bing scored and ranked, participants can now decide which they want to tackle now, soon, or later.

Training exercise:

Matrix scoring

Purpose: To introduce and practise matrix scoring.

Time: One and a half-hours.

Materials: A large copy or overhead transparency of FIGURE 26 and any others you may have. Flipchart paper and thick pens if needed.

Steps
1 Explain what matrix scoring is and how it can be used. Ask people to share any experiences they have of using this technique. Show the example given above and discuss it. Show any other examples you may have.
2 In small groups (with a facilitator, observer and note-taker) ask participants to think about six items linked to an issue which interests them and write them down or use pictures or objects to represent them across the top of a matrix. Then they need to discuss and identify about six criteria for judging the importance of these items and to write these down the left-hand side of the matrix as shown in the example opposite.

3 Ask each person to mark dots on a piece of paper (or collect about 20 stones or beans) for each criterion and divide them among the items on the basis of their ranking for each criterion in turn. For example, they will give fewer stones (or dots) to the criteria they rank lower and more to those they rank higher.
4 When all the dots or stones have been placed ask each group to add up the scores and then to rank the issues in order of importance.
5 When all the groups have finished, walk around together to visit each matrix. Ask the facilitator to explain their matrix and give reasons for their choices. Ask the observer to comment on the group process and ask the note-taker to make a permanent record of the matrix on paper. Invite people to make comments and ask questions.

Well-being ranking

Please note that this technique needs to be used with caution in some communities because relative wealth or poverty is a sensitive topic and people may not wish their status to be publicly displayed. For this reason it may need to be carried out in a private setting. This technique has sometimes proved problematic in urban areas, where people tend to be less familiar with their neighbours than in rural communities. The results of the wealth ranking should be cross-checked by using other techniques such as social mapping.

What is it?

Well-being ranking is a technique that can be used to interpret the relative well-being of members of a community or a group based on local views and criteria. It is also known as wealth ranking. It is easier to gather information on relative values regarding people's wealth than to get absolute figures by asking questions like 'How much do you earn?' Identifying those households that are the poorest and most vulnerable in the community can help to make sure that they are not 'invisible' and forgotten when carrying out a needs assessment.

How is it used?

To conduct a well-being ranking the group of participants starts by writing the name of the head of each household on a card. Then they identify the criteria by which they are going to assess the well-being of a household and decide how many categories of well-being they want to have. For example they may decide on four categories – highest and lowest and two in the middle range. The facilitator then reads out the name of each head of household and the group discusses and agrees which category of well-being this household should be placed in.

Once the participants have finished the card sorting, the facilitator asks them to go back and check the piles and make any changes they wish. When the participants are content with the results the facilitator can ask questions to find out more about, for example, the factors determining a household's place in the ranking and what could lead to a household moving from one wealth group to another. It is also useful for participants to identify two or three 'typical' households within each wealth group, which the planners can visit at a later stage. A record is kept of the characteristics of households in each wealth group and, where appropriate, the names of the households in each group. It is recommended that this technique is carried out with at least three groups of participants for every 100 households. It is good to have men and women in different groups because men and women often use very different criteria for deciding on well-being.

From experience:

Wealth ranking in Jumbe village, Eastern Province, Zambia.

During a needs assessment exercise in Jumbe village the planning team decided that information was needed on which of the thirteen households in the village were well off and which were poor. To generate this information a member of the planning team worked with a local man who knew each household well. The man started by writing the name of the head of each household on a card. He decided that the households could be divided into three groups. He then sorted the cards into these three groups using the different characteristics described below to decide which group to put a card into.

Group 1
'Nchaska' – those who are 'not in a bad state'. This group had five households, all male-headed, and all linked through relatives of the mother. These households had the following characteristics:

- most of them sell tobacco,
- they have all lived and worked in town,
- they are all relatively well educated,
- one man owns a building he rents as a shop,
- the houses are larger, made from better materials.

To be rich, this group would need fertiliser, loans, and tractor hire facilities.

Group 2
This group had seven households – three male-headed, four female-headed. These households had the following characteristics:

- most rely on making mats for extra income,
- there are three female-headed households,
- they have problems in getting money because they do not plan,
- they do not produce very much from their farms.

To improve their situation, 'they don't need help from anyone, they just need to help themselves'.

Group 3

Muleme Banda is the only person in this category. She lives on her own and has no children or husband. She is old and cannot do basic domestic tasks like carrying water. She is often without food, and depends on charity and relatives for survival. She does grow some sorghum. To improve her situation she needs combined village assistance (money) to buy essentials like salt and food. She also needs help in drawing her water, thatching her house and other major jobs.

This exercise was then done again. This time a woman from the community was asked to rank the same households. She sorted the cards into four groups. She placed the same households into the wealthiest group as the previous sorter had done. She also had only Muleme Banda in the poorest group. She divided the other households into two groups. She would not say how she had decided on the breakdown.

This wealth ranking exercise showed how the situation of the really poor person was regarded as a matter for the community – not for outside assistance. The situation of the intermediate group was regarded as one of self-help. The situation of the relatively well off was regarded as one that outside agencies could help to solve. A strong correlation emerged between isolated women (no husband or living children) and 'core' poverty.

(Source: Adapted from the World Bank (1994), *Zambia Poverty Assessment Report No. 12985-ZA, Vol. V: Participatory Poverty Assessment*, Southern Africa Department, Human Resources Division, Washington, D.C.)

Training exercise:

Wealth ranking

Purpose: To introduce and practise well-being ranking.

Time: One and a half-hours.

Materials: A large copy or overhead transparency of the example of well-being ranking made using the description above and any others you may have. Twenty small cards and a pen. Flipchart paper and pens if needed.

Steps

1 Explain what well-being ranking is and how it can be used.
2 Ask participants what techniques (if any) they have already used to explore relative wealth or well-being. Also ask them to say how they have decided whether people are well off or not, for example, the poor, the land-less, female-headed households, etc.
3 Show the example given above and any others you may have and discuss them.
4 Organise a role-play as a fishbowl exercise. You can do this by inviting about four or five volunteers to take part in a role-play in the centre of the training area. Ask the rest of the participants to sit in a circle around them to observe what they are doing.
5 Start by asking one volunteer (preferably someone who has experience of doing well-being ranking) to role play a project worker and the rest of the volunteers to role-play local people.

In the role play the project worker starts by telling the local people that he or she has come to do an activity with them called well-being ranking and explains what it is all about. He or she then facilitates the group whilst they carry out a well-being ranking of the households in their community as described above under the heading 'How is it used?' The project worker will need about 20 cards and a pen to write down the name of each head of household to be sorted. He or she will also need to distinguish between different categories of well-being. (We have used piles of shoes to do this – the more shoes in the pile the higher the category of well-being.)

After the role-play invite the role-players and the observers to make comments and ask questions. Emphasise that in some communities, relative wealth and poverty is a very sensitive topic, and this technique may need to be conducted in a private setting to allow participants to talk freely. Stress that in some cases, the technique should be avoided.

4.2   Flow charts

What are they?

Flow charts are diagrams that show the causes or consequences of a problem and the relationships or linkages between them. For example, they can be useful to show the causes or results of drunkenness in a community. They can also be used to show the results of major changes such as introducing rice into a maize growing region. In this case they are known as *impact diagrams*. They can also be used to show how farm and livelihood systems (ways of earning a living) are linked. In this case they are called *systems diagrams*.

How are they used?

Flow charts are used to find out why local people are not always able to improve their lives and solve problems. Identifying the many different causes of a problem helps people understand how they can change themselves and what changes need to be made within their family and community. An example of a flow chart showing the many causes of teenage pregnancy is given below.

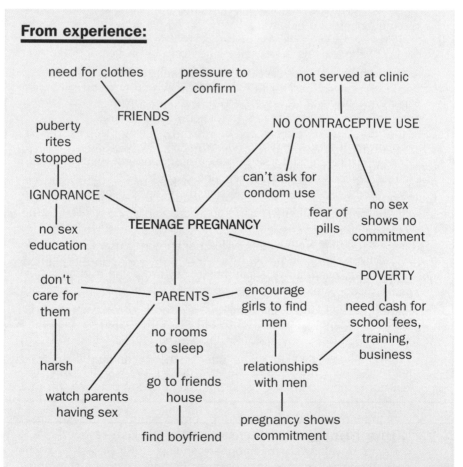

From experience:

FIGURE 27   Flow chart drawn by young women in Ghana showing causes of teenage pregnancy

(*Source*: Gill Gordon and Planned Parenthood Association of Ghana.)

Identifying the results of problems can also help people to change their behaviour and improve their living conditions. If people become more aware of the forces that influence their lives and their behaviour they can think of ways to change these forces. As a result they can more easily carry out behaviours that result in happy and healthy relationships and improved well-being.

Training exercise:

Flow charts

Purpose: To introduce and practise flow charts to show the causes and consequences of problems.

Time: Two hours.

Materials: A large copy or overhead transparency of the example of the flow chart given in FIGURE 27 and any others you may have. Flipchart paper and pens, chalk and chalkboard.

Steps
1 Explain what flow charts are and how they are used.
2 Divide participants into single sex groups and ask each group to select a facilitator, observer and note-taker. Encourage the facilitator to start the process and then 'hand over the stick' to another group member. (By this we mean handing over the role of facilitator.)
3 Ask each group to choose a problem linked to their own behaviour that they would all like to solve (such as overworking, stress, lack of exercise, overeating). Explain that they are going to draw a flow chart to show all the causes of this problem and how they are linked together. This can also be called a *causal diagram*.
4 Explain that they should start by asking 'But why do we have this problem?' Stress that people should not be satisfied with the immediate causes that they write down first of all. They should keep on asking themselves 'But why does this happen?' until they run out of new ideas. By doing this they can get down to the root causes of the problem.
5 Give them the following example: If someone puts on the flow chart 'drunkenness is caused by tiredness' and you just leave it there, it does not develop very much understanding. But if we ask 'But why does tiredness lead to drunkenness?' then we learn something more. We can keep asking 'But why?' after each answer until people do not have any more answers left and we have learned as much as we can.

6 If possible get some of the groups to work outside, drawing their flow charts on the ground using local objects. Get other groups to use chalk on a concrete floor or blackboard.

7 When the groups have finished their flow charts ask them to draw a second flow chart to show the consequences of their problem.

8 When the flow charts are finished bring the whole group together and walk around, visiting each flow chart in turn. Ask each group to explain their flow charts and then invite questions and comments. Ask: What are the main causes of the problem? How could you as individuals or as a group help to reduce the problem? Are there any differences between the charts drawn by men and women?

9 Lead a discussion on how the process of drawing the flowcharts went. Ask: How well did the team members (facilitators, note-takers, observers and others) work together in our group? Did the facilitator remember to 'hand over the stick' or did certain people dominate? How well were you able to put different ideas together in the diagram? How much time did you need to develop a useful flow chart? If you had been working with local people how would the process have been different? What are the good things and bad things about this method? What other methods could we use to look at causes and effects of problems? (Other methods often used are role-plays and stories.)

10 Explain that these flow charts can be used again when the group wants to look at ways of solving the problem. Ask the note-takers to copy the flow charts onto paper if they have been drawn on the ground or on the floor or blackboard, so that they will have a copy if they need it later on.

11 Summarise and close the session.

4.3   Draw-and-write

What is it?

Draw-and-write is a technique where people draw pictures and write about what is happening in their pictures. The technique is sometimes called drawing-and-dialogue to emphasise that the pictures are most useful when used to start discussion. These pictures, together with the writing, help us to understand better how different people (including children) view their world. Drawing pictures can help people to break down barriers and allow powerful emotions to be expressed. The draw-and-write technique can give information that is more useful than written information only. Draw-and-write also helps people who are not very literate, because they can do the drawing and then ask for help in writing down what they want to say, or they can discuss their drawing without any writing.

How is it used?

We can use this technique to help us understand how people view their world. It can be used in many different situations but it has been mostly used to help us understand how children view health, illness and disease (see Further reading in Appendix 1). We can learn more from this technique if we ask people to discuss their pictures.

From experience:

The draw-and-write technique

Children in Botswana were asked to draw pictures about the things most people die from in their community and to write about the pictures. The pictures fell into six main categories – disease, violence, accidents, wild animals, suicide, unhealthy habits and witchcraft. Some of the pictures they drew are shown below.

FIGURE 28   The draw-and-write technique

<u>Training exercise:</u>

The draw-and-write technique

Purpose: To introduce and practise the draw-and-write technique.

Time: One and a half hours.

Materials: A large copy or overhead transparency of FIGURE 28 or any other examples you may have. Plain paper and pencils or pens.

Steps:

1 Explain what the draw-and-write technique is and how it can be used. Ask people to share any experiences they have of using this technique. Show the example given above and discuss it. Show any other examples you may have.

2 Give each participant a sheet of plain paper and ask them to draw a picture of a healthy person who is the same age and sex as themselves and to write about what that person can do to keep themselves healthy.

3 When they have finished, hand out a second sheet of plain paper and ask them to draw a picture of an unhealthy (sick) person who is the same age and sex as themselves and to write about what that person could have done to make themselves unhealthy.

4 Display the drawings in two groups – 'healthy' and 'unhealthy'. Ask participants to look at what people have written about keeping healthy and find the main categories of response such as i) eating good food or ii) taking regular exercise. Do this exercise again using the 'unhealthy' pictures. Discuss the findings.

5 Finally encourage people to ask questions and make comments about the draw-and-write activity. What did they like about it? What did they not like about it? Explain that encouraging people to discuss their views about the activity is important because drawing can make people feel very emotional. The facilitator therefore needs to give people a chance to talk about these emotions before they leave.

4.4   Drama and Forum Theatre

What is it?

Drama techniques involve people in developing and acting out a situation. Acting in front of an audience is called theatre. When people are invited from the audience to participate actively in the drama it is called Forum Theatre or

Participatory Educational Theatre (PET). In Forum Theatre the actors are also trained as educators. It is most effective if these actors are people from the community. We can use Forum Theatre to raise awareness about gender issues and inequalities and help people gain a better understanding of how the world around them works and how they can improve their lives. This approach to theatre uses the ideas from the book *'Theatre of the Oppressed'* written by Augusto Boal. These ideas have a lot in common with the ideas expressed by Paulo Freire in his book *Pedagogy of the Oppressed* discussed in Chapter 1.

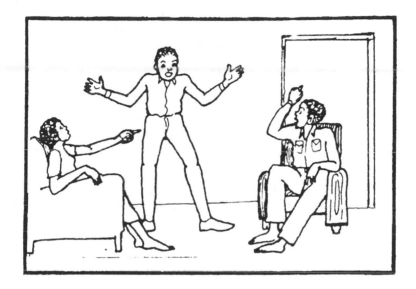

FIGURE 29   Drama and Forum Theatre

How is it used?

In Forum Theatre the facilitator acts as an intermediary between the actors and the audience. The way that this happens is described below. There is also an observer and note-taker. The facilitator starts by introducing the play to the audience. There are usually only two or three actors and they perform a number of short scenes to show a problem, which has already been identified by the community. They do not show the solution.

For example, if teenage pregnancy has been identified as a problem by local people the drama may start with a stranger driving into the community and parking near to the school gates. This driver is a middle-aged man dressed in a smart suit; he lives in the city. After a while he sees a teenage girl coming out of school. He opens the car door and introduces himself as a friend of her father. He tells her to get into the car and says he will take her for a delicious meal at a local restaurant. She looks worried and is not sure what to do but then decides to get into the car and go with him. The next scene could show her in distress being comforted by a friend.

When all the scenes have been performed the facilitator asks the audience questions to check they have understood the problem shown. He or she then invites members of the audience to come up and interview each of the actors to find out more about the problem. For example, the first interviewer may ask the rich man 'Why did you drive into our community? Did you come looking for our daughters?' The second interviewer may ask the girl 'Why did this rich man offer you a lift in his car? What did he want? Why did you agree to go with him?' This type of interviewing is known as 'hot seating' the actors.

In Forum Theatre the play is then run again. But this time the facilitator encourages members of the audience to stop the play when they see a chance for the person being oppressed (in this case the young girl) to change the course of events. The facilitator then invites the person who has stopped the play to take over the role of the young girl and change the script so that the girl does not agree to get into the rich man's car. In PET the role of any of the actors can be taken over by members of the audience with the aim of changing what happens next.

The facilitator summarises what they have all learned about why this problem is happening in their community. He or she then asks people to suggest what they can do to solve it and leads a discussion about each suggestion that is made. This final discussion is the most important part of the learning process and it needs to be given plenty of time.

Before the end of the day the planning team come together to get feedback from the observer and the note-taker. They discuss, summarise and record all the information that has been generated by the Forum Theatre. (You can read more about the use of drama for participatory planning from PLA Notes No. 29 in the list of Further reading given in Appendix 1.)

From experience:

Participatory Educational Theatre in Mbabane village, Kenya

During a participatory needs assessment conducted for the community-based nutrition programme in Kenya, members of the community in one village agreed that family disagreements were a problem. The planning team then developed a play to show this problem but not to give solutions. Each scene was developed around a central question (as shown below). One team member was the facilitator and there was also an observer and a note-taker.

At their next meeting with the community the team performed the play. The facilitator welcomed the audience and told them that the play was about the problem of family disagreements that people had agreed was a problem for them at the last community meeting. The facilitator then showed them a large copy of the central question for the first scene and read it out to the audience. The play then started.

Scene 1: Mr Nyaga is leaving the house to sell miraa (a locally grown crop containing stimulants). As he goes out his wife shouts at him 'Our son is sick. I have to take him to the clinic. Our maize meal is finished. We have nothing to eat for dinner.' Her husband is angry. He asks 'What have you done with all the maize we had? Did you give it away to your friends? Did you sell it?' He goes out slamming the door behind him and his wife turns to the audience, crying 'What am I going to do? He treats me so badly. I feel so unhappy.'
Central question: Why is it difficult for the husband and wife to sit down and talk about the household problems?

Scene 2: A neighbour enters the house to try to borrow some money from Mr Nyaga. He is an irresponsible, lazy person. Mrs Nyaga 'Why do you come here asking for money? Why do you think my husband has money to give you?' He says 'I know your husband has money. He has just been paid for harvesting sand.'Mrs Nyaga did not know about this work. She is angry that the neighbour has come to borrow money. She says 'It is neighbours like you who ruin my husband.' When her husband comes home she asks him angrily about this money: 'So you have kept money away from me and we have nothing to eat.'He goes out slamming the door again.
Central question: Why did Mr Nyaga tell his friend about the work but not his wife?

When the play was finished the facilitator asked the audience what they saw. He then used the two central questions to stimulate discussion about the problem. Members of the audience were invited to interview (hot-seat) Mr and Mrs Nyaga to learn more about the reasons for their disagreements. This highlighted important differences in power and access to resources between men and women in this society. The play was then run again but this time members of the audience were invited to stop the play when they wanted to take over the roles of Mr or Mrs Nyaga so that they were able to talk about the household problems.

Finally, the facilitator summarised the causes of family disagreements in the village and led a discussion about the possible solutions that had been suggested.

From experience:

A scenario developed for using Participatory Educational Theatre with a sexual health training project in Dhaka

Scene 1: In a drop-in centre in Dhaka for sex workers two women are sitting in the centre, Shareen (a sex worker) is learning how to use the sewing machine. Amena, who is a project outreach worker, is sitting on the floor resting. Shareen asks Amena to let her have some condoms and tells her that she thinks she has an STD. Amena gives her some condoms and advises her to go to see the doctor when she comes to the centre that afternoon. Shareen doesn't go to the doctor that day. *Central question: Why was it difficult for Shareen to go to see the doctor?*

Scene 2: The same night on the street near the drop-in centre. Shareen is hoping to get a rich client and when one comes up she starts to negotiate the price with him. They go round the corner and she tries to persuade him to use a condom but he refuses. She offers him non-penetrative sex but when he gets angry she is frightened and gives in. *Central question: Why was it difficult for Shareen to persuade her client to use a condom?*

Scene 3: Three months later in the drop-in centre, Amena is sewing and Shareen is lying on the floor looking very sick. Shareen still has the STD symptoms but is now getting fever and diarrhoea. Amena goes with her to see the doctor who advises her to use condoms with her clients and takes some blood to test.

Scene 4: Two weeks later in the drop-in centre Amena finds Shareen lying on the floor in the drop-in centre, she is crying. She has been to see the doctor – she has caught HIV.

The facilitator introduced the scenes and when the play was finished he asked the audience what they had seen happening. He then used the central questions to stimulate discussion about the problem. Members of the audience were invited to interview (hot-seat) the actors to learn more about the problem. The play was then run again but this time members of the audience were invited to stop the play when they wanted to take over the role of any of the actors and change the script so that Shareen did not catch HIV.

Training exercise:

Drama techniques

Purpose: To develop and perform Forum Theatre or PET.

Time: One day.

Steps:

1 Explain what Forum Theatre and PET are and how they can be used.

2 In small groups ask participants to tell each other a real-life story from their own experience that ends up with someone being oppressed. Explain that people have to trust each other to tell personal stories and they must agree to keep their discussions confidential. However, it is difficult to guarantee confidentiality in a group and people may prefer to tell a story as if it happened to someone else. Tell them that after listening to each other's stories they should choose one of the stories to develop as a drama.

3 To develop the drama ask each group to identify two or three key points in their story. They will develop each scene of the play around one of these key points. The first step is to use themselves as actors to make a snapshot or frozen picture to show each of the key points. For example, in the story given previously about the teenage girl and the rich man, the snapshots might be as follows: Snapshot one: Rich man leaning against his car smoking a cigarette and grinning at schoolgirl who is looking back worriedly over her shoulder at him. Snapshot two: Schoolgirl crying and friend comforting her.

4 Each group then shows their snapshots in turn to the whole group. Then ask the group to say what they have seen in the tableau and to say what the key points being shown were.

5 Ask each group to turn their snapshots into role-plays and show them to the group as before. When people are giving feedback on the role-plays it is important that they make useful comments, starting with what they thought was good before giving suggestions on how it could be further improved. Allow time for the groups to develop the role-plays into the final scenes of the play and to rehearse the scenes.

6 Finally, ask each group to present their play to the whole group and to receive useful comments. Discuss the good points of each play and help the group to choose one of the plays to perform as Forum Theatre.

7 Explain that the play they have chosen is now going to be run again but that this time they should stop the play and take the place of the character being oppressed when they see a chance for the script to

be changed and the problem avoided. Select a facilitator, observer and note-taker.

8 Lead a discussion to share what people learned from the play. Start by inviting the facilitator, observer and note-taker to give feedback to the group on how the play went, who participated and who did not. Then invite the rest of the group to ask questions and make comments on what they have learned: What were the key issues and conflicts in the play? When people took over the role of the actor and changed the script, were the changes they made realistic or 'magical'? How could the play be changed to make it better if it was going to be run again?

Notes

1 Ranking means placing items in order of priority, and scoring gives different values to each item according to its rank. For example, the item ranked first may get ten points, the items ranked second nine points and so on.

5 Doing a participatory needs assessment

The previous three chapters have described methods and techniques used to generate information and give opportunities for empowerment. This chapter gives a step-by-step description of how these methods can be used, by professionals who are relatively new to participatory approaches, to conduct a needs assessment. The approach given can help professionals move away from just taking information from people, towards giving them some opportunities for empowerment.

5.1   What is a participatory needs assessment?

To start the planning process it is necessary to find out what is needed in the community and how these needs can best be met. All too often in the past, this assessment of needs has been made by professionals on behalf of the people who will benefit from the programme. Based on their training and experience, professionals have presumed that they know what is best for local people who do not have their professional background. The results have often been a disaster. A frequently quoted example is the aid provided by the Soviet Union to assist Ghana to build an airport. Professional knowledge and experience sent snowploughs to a tropical country! In order to overcome problems like this, planners are now emphasising the need for more participatory needs assessments.

These experiences are relatively new. Much of the early work was motivated by the need for planners to get accurate information that could be quickly generated and used.

A **participatory needs assessment** is the first step in a process in which professionals and local people form a partnership to identify community needs, set priorities and develop a long-term plan of action to meet these needs.

The needs assessment presented below is an example developed for the World Health Organisation (WHO). It shows how a participatory planning process can be started to improve services for the poor and to build partnerships between professionals/planners and community people. This approach to needs assessment has been used by many groups, in both resource-rich and resource-poor countries, to begin the participatory process. It is a useful way of:

- helping professionals and agency people understand the situation in the communities in which they want to work,
- encouraging change in attitudes, behaviour and practices of professionals, agencies and larger institutions, such as ministries of health and education, that are committed to using more participatory ways of working,
- finding ways in which professionals, who work in rigid bureaucratic organisations, can become more open and flexible to meet community needs,
- building alliances among professional and local people to allow opportunities for empowerment of community people,
- providing opportunities for professionals to learn from, and experience the value of participatory approaches,
- enabling professionals to put into practice the skills, methods and techniques that encourage successful partnerships to develop,
- allowing professionals to gain confidence in the ability of local people to make substantial contributions to the planning process.

To carry out a needs assessment we can follow the nine steps described below. This helps us to be systematic in our approach and helps to make sure our objectives will be achieved. To be successful the assessment must involve people in a way that makes the best use of all resources and works toward a realistic plan of action.

Guidelines for steps for doing a participatory needs assessment

1 Reviewing the existing support.
2 Assessing the available resources.
3 Preparing the assessment team.
4 Deciding what information is needed.
5 Deciding how to get the information and who will get it.
6 Collecting the information.
7 Analysing the information.
8 Reviewing the information with all needs assessment participants.
9 Defining priorities and developing a plan of action.

5.2   Reviewing the existing support

The first step is to find out if participatory approaches are likely to succeed. We need to consider carefully:

- how stable the political situation is,
- how much support there is for participation within our own organisation(s),
- what we can do to strengthen the support and overcome barriers to participation (for example, we could hold a seminar to raise awareness of the need for participation),
- whether government and local authorities are promoting participation and providing support for it,
- what we can do to develop people's skills in facilitating groups, in taking leadership and in helping groups to build agreement and make decisions.

We can conduct a SWOT analysis to help us consider the situation in an organised way. A SWOT analysis is an exercise in which we try to identify the Strengths, Weaknesses, Opportunities and Threats, which may help or prevent participation in the planning process. We can use a SWOT analysis on our own or with other members of the team. This analysis helps us to think about building on our strengths. It also makes us aware of the opportunities we have for participation.

From experience:

A SWOT analysis in Naibasti village, India

A local politician in Bombay, India was coming up for re-election. In the hope of gaining votes from people living in Naibasti, one of the shanty town areas near the airport, he invited the social worker who lived and worked in the area to attend a meeting of the Bombay Municipal Council. He suggested that the Council members might be willing to give some money to improve the living conditions in Naibasti if he could come up with a good plan. To develop such a plan the social worker invited the teacher from the women's literacy class, a local trader and the head of the women's union to join him as members of a planning team. At their first meeting, the team decided to ask the Municipal Council to give them some small funding to involve members of the Naibasti community in a participatory needs assessment exercise. They also decided to ask the Council to allow them to come back again when the community had developed an action plan. To help them understand their position better they conducted a SWOT analysis. Here are some of the things they thought about:

Their strengths: The social worker had been trained in using participatory approaches to needs assessment and had experience of facilitating it. Other members of the team also had skills in promoting leadership and helping groups build agreement and make decisions.

They had support from the local politician who was very friendly with two of the council members. There was support from the Minister of Health for participation as he had recently published a newspaper article calling on citizens to participate actively in improving their own lives.

Their weaknesses: The team members could not speak all the languages spoken in the community. Involving the community in planning went against the tradition of experts designing projects and viewing community members simply as users of health services and providers of labour for construction projects.

The opportunities they could build on: They had been given the chance to present their case to the Municipal Council. There was going to be an international conference on child health in Bombay in six months time and the delegates could be invited to visit Naibasti to help promote the work they were doing to improve health.

The threats they would face: Some members of the Municipal Council would be opposed to the idea of helping the Naibasti community to become empowered. Some powerful traders in the next shantytown area would be jealous of any support given to Naibasti by the Municipal Council.

After identifying these strengths, weaknesses, opportunities and threats the team decided how best to build on their strengths, use the opportunities, overcome their weaknesses and deal with the threats. They decided to recruit local people from each language group to help translate during the needs assessment and to ask the local politician to help them influence the Council members. They would convince the Council that they needed to involve local people from the start, to give the planned activities a better chance of continuing over time.

Training exercise:

Doing a SWOT analysis

Purpose: To introduce and conduct a SWOT analysis.

Time: One and a half hours.

Materials: Flipchart paper and thick pens.

Steps:
1 Write the first letters of each topic (SWOT) on flipchart paper and ask

the participants if they know, or can guess, what the letters stand for. Provide any extra explanation needed.

2 Explain that once we have decided on a course of action we can use a SWOT analysis to help us understand how best to achieve our aims. For example, if we want to introduce a participatory approach to planning into our workplace we need to know how to build on our strengths, overcome our weaknesses, use any opportunities we have and avoid any threats to carrying out our plan of action.

3 In small groups ask the participants to do a SWOT analysis to discuss the strengths, weaknesses, opportunities and threats each of them would face if they wanted to use a participatory approach to project planning. The following questions can be used to guide their discussion. Ask each group to choose one member's SWOT analysis to present to the whole group.

Strengths
- What experience and skills do we already have in our team for participatory planning?
- Who are our friends and allies in support of participation?
- What arguments can we make for wanting to adopt a participatory approach to planning?
- What current ideas within our own organisation can we build on to promote the use of a participatory approach?
- In what way does the current political policy or plan at government and local levels support participatory approaches?
- Are there any managers or politicians who may support a participatory approach?
- Who stands to benefit from the participatory approach and how will they benefit?
- What arguments can we use to strengthen their support for participation?

Weaknesses
- Are there any managers or politicians who are opposed to a participatory approach to planning?
- In what way is the current policy or plan preventing participation?
- How can this lack of support be overcome?
    1) What arguments could we use to promote participation?
    2) How can the critical skills needed for facilitating groups and for participatory decision-making be developed?

Opportunities
- What opportunities can we use to support participation? For example, are there statements from international organisations, from government, NGOs or local newspapers to support participation?

- What national or local initiatives can we join up with to help support participation? (For example, national campaigns or tours by local politicians.)

Threats
- Who are our enemies – who are likely to oppose participation?
- Who stands to lose from the use of a participatory approach?
- How can we bring these people on board to reduce the threat they pose?
- How can we set up a 'win-win' situation in which everyone gets something that they want out of supporting participation? For example, a situation where a district medical officer agrees to join a participatory needs assessment team in order to get increased uptake of health services and the community gets an opportunity to participate in planning the provision of services to meet its needs.

Invite each group to give feedback on their discussions.

5.3   Assessing the available resources

We also need to think about resources. Participatory planning, like other types of planning, needs to consider what resources are needed and how any shortfall in resources can be overcome. The most important resources include:

- *People:* We need to think about who is going to be involved in planning. This will include professionals and local people who are members of the planning team and, if necessary, representatives of the local authorities. Each person needs to be identified by name. What they are expected to contribute to the planning process must also be clearly stated.
- *Time:* We need to consider how much time the first assessment of needs will take. (Remember the process of planning programmes is like a spiral and we will need to go back and reassess needs during the process.) Planning will continue after the first needs assessment has been carried out because information from monitoring and evaluation will become available and be used to review and adjust the plan. We will need to make decisions about how long it will take to generate enough information to start the programme. We will also need to decide how much time each person is expected to spend on the programme. This calculation includes time spent by both professionals and local people.
- *Space:* We need to decide where the assessment will be done? If group discussions are going to be held, we need to find places where meetings can take place. If special groups, such as teachers or health workers are going to be involved, meeting rooms will need to be found. If a team of professionals and local people are going to generate and interpret the information

together we need to find space for them to work on the information and to store the results. We will need to book a big hall and make a timetable for meetings at which we can report the results of the assessment to the whole community.

• *Cost:* We need to think about how much the assessment will cost? We will need to include the cost of professional and local people's time. While both may give their time free of charge as a mark of their commitment to the programme, we need to be aware of its actual cost. We also need to calculate the cost of materials such as pens, paper and other stationery, as well as computer use. We need to think about transport costs. We also need to think about subsistence payments to professionals who do field work and to local people who provide hospitality for visitors to the programme.

5.4   Preparing the assessment team

The next step in conducting a participatory needs assessment is to build a team of key people from various professions and trades. The professionals in this team are likely to be from different backgrounds and experiences. The team must then prepare itself to meet the two main aims of the assessment exercise. These aims are:

1 To generate the information needed to identify the priority needs from the point of view of the community members and to develop a plan of action to meet these needs.
2 To create opportunities for community members, particularly the poor and powerless, to gain skills and experience to make choices and act on plans about their future.

These aims must be kept in mind throughout the assessment process. To achieve these aims, team members need to understand the methods for generating information. They also need to develop the attitudes, skills and confidence to work with the community and with each other in a participatory way. A four-day workshop at the beginning of the planning exercise is one way to help support these efforts. This workshop should include sessions on exploring attitudes and improving listening and speaking skills and on the use of qualitative methods for generating information.[1] It should also include some sessions on using quantitative methods for making a basic profile of the community. This profile can include information on the number of men, women and children of different ages in the community, ethnic groups, languages spoken, livelihoods, adult literacy rate, infant mortality rate,[2] staple foods and levels of child malnutrition.

After the training workshop the team will meet to discuss how to do a participatory planning exercise. To allow all members of the planning team to have opportunities to contribute to this discussion we can use the VIPP (Visualisation in Participatory Programmes) method described in Chapter 2, section 6. VIPP also helps develop a climate that encourages participation and can support the planning exercise.

5.5   Deciding what information is needed

To help us decide what information is needed and avoid collecting more information than is necessary we can use the diagram given below. This diagram is called an information pyramid.

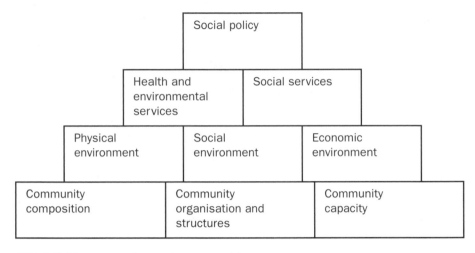

FIGURE 30   The information pyramid

(*Source:* Annett, Hugh and Rifkin, Susan B., *Guidelines for rapid participatory appraisals to assess community health needs*, Geneva: WHO/SHS/DHS/95.8)

The headings in each of the building blocks of the pyramid help us decide what sort of information is needed to understand the situation of people living in a specific location. The pyramid has three important features:

• It is based on needs identified by the community.
• It is built on information generated from documents, from dialogue between professionals and community members, and from observations.
• It reflects the situation at a given point in time and recognises that communities are rapidly changing.

The bottom level of the pyramid describes the community. For example, its composition (the number of people, their age and sex, the ethnic groups, and other identifying characteristics), community organisation and structures (local organisations – government and non-government, groups working in the community) and community capacity (evidence of working together to carry out community projects such as building a community centre or organising to press government to meet local needs). Because the planning process is based on community involvement and contribution to any plan of action, the planning team must have a detailed understanding of the community with whom they are working. It will be necessary to find out the strengths and weaknesses of the community leadership, organisations and structures.

The second level of the pyramid describes the things that influence the community sense of well-being. For example, the physical environment (location, climate, housing, transportation, communications, etc), social environment (level of education, existing welfare support) and economic environment (sources of income, level of income, access to food, housing, employment). We need this information to find out what improvement is possible and what are the barriers to this improvement. Information on the physical environment helps to identify problems related to overcrowding, pollution and access to services. Information on social aspects looks at traditional beliefs and values that help or hinder change. Economic information describes income sources, earning potential and the economic opportunities for various groups.

The third level of the pyramid describes information on the existence, coverage, accessibility and acceptability of social services. This includes information on health services, environmental services such as water and waste disposal, education, and support for socially disadvantaged people including the disabled.

The top level of the pyramid describes information on national, regional and local social policies for improving the situation of people who are poor and disadvantaged. Information on policy will tell us whether the political leadership is committed to improving the lives of poor people. With strong government support at both the top and local levels, improvements for these people can proceed more rapidly and without major political barriers.

Experience gained by rapid appraisals can help us to make best use of the information pyramid. Rapid Rural Appraisal (RRA) and Participatory Rapid/Rural Appraisal (PRA) experiences have highlighted the need to generate only the information that is absolutely relevant and necessary. Information should not be generated just because it is available. There is no point in quickly generating large amounts of information that will then need a lot of time to interpret. For example, we would not want to do a household survey to generate information on the number of malnourished children, if malnutrition was not identified by the community as a major problem.

In the field, the assessment team will collect information about these four levels to build the pyramid. The pyramid shape reminds the team that success depends on building a planning process that rests on strong community involvement at the base. In addition, it reminds the team that the amount of information needed about each block in the pyramid is relative to its position on the pyramid – this means that more information is needed about the community than about social policy. It is the *accuracy* and *usefulness* of the information and not the *amount* of information that is most crucial.

The blocks in the information pyramid help us decide what sort of information is needed. Again, using the VIPP method, the team writes key words on cards to represent a topic on which they want information. For example, topics may be sources of water, food availability, availability of schools and health services.

A facilitator helps the team to examine each card to see if information on this topic is easy to get and can be used immediately to develop a plan of action. If the information can be used immediately and is also easy to get then the team accepts the card and it is placed in one of the pyramid blocks. In this way, the team reaches agreement on what topics are most important for generating information. These cards are the basis of a checklist of topics, which each team member will use in doing the needs assessment. To help us identify where to find the information, different coloured cards can be used. For example, if we first look for information in documents we can write the topic on a yellow card, for interviews on blue cards and for observations on green cards.

From experience:

Needs assessment in Tanzania

Officials from the municipal council of Mbeya, Tanzania, participated in a ten-day workshop to prepare themselves to do a needs assessment. On day two of the workshop, the information pyramid was explored in detail. Participants were divided into three teams composed of members from different sectors of the government. They remained in these teams throughout the entire exercise. Each team was asked to brainstorm questions (the first questions that come into their minds) that they needed to build the blocks of the pyramid. Using coloured cards they wrote key words to identify topics they wished to collect information about. The facilitators read each card, then the entire group decided which block the card was to be placed in. The pyramid had been drawn on large sheets of flipchart paper and displayed on a wall. These blocks provided the basis for the checklist for information collection. This checklist showed which topics the team felt were important to gather information on.

From experience:

An example of a checklist for needs assessment created by the Mbeya Muncipal Council, Tanzania

1 Social policy
Legislation.
National policies for health, education and social welfare.

2 Health and environmental services
Availability of health services (including traditional medicines).
Availability of environmental services.
Availability of clean water.
Existence of sanitation services (garbage collection, etc.).

3 Social services
Accessibility to schooling.
Availability of child care.
Services which are missing (recreational, markets, disability services).

4 Physical environment
Adequacy of housing.
Adequacy of roads/transport.
Water/waste disposal.
Excreta disposal.
Common diseases.
Causes of death.

5 Social environment
Availability of food/ essential commodities.
Kinds of community support systems (church, social organisations).

6 Economic environment
Level of income.
Sources of income.

7 Community composition
Differences (tribes, politics, income).
Age/sex/population.
Birth and death rates.
Cultural commonalities and differences.

8 Community organisation
Local government organisation.
Existence of Non-Government Organisations (NGOs).

9 Community capacities
Self-help projects.
Participation in development projects.
Projects which have been sustained by the community.

To collect the information each team member needs to have a notebook that serves as the logbook. To help record information the pages can be divided into two equal sections. On the left side, information which is generated from interviews can be written down. On the right side information generated from observations can be written down.

5.6   Deciding how to get the information and who will get it

To get information, which is useful and generated quickly, we can start by talking to key informants. Key informants are people in the community who, because of their position as formal or informal leaders, have information about community problems rather than individual problems. For this reason, they can be seen as representatives of a range of opinions that the community holds.

Guidelines for identifying who are key informants?
1 Local government officials.
2 Informal community leaders.
3 Social and health service personnel.
4 Teachers.
5 Religious leaders.
6 Chairpeople of local organisations.
7 Women's groups leaders.
8 Owners of local businesses.
9 Members of non-governmental organisations working in the area.

Remember!
This list is only an example. It must be changed according to your own situation.

In choosing key informants it is important that the team identifies people who are members of the marginalised groups in the community. These groups rarely get represented in community projects. If teams do not involve people from these groups, both the quality of information and the process of empowerment are put in danger. For example, it is important to make sure that women and children are included, because men are usually seen to have more information or are more aggressive about giving information.

In working with key informants, the team needs to decide what the relationship will be and how informants can be brought into the information generation process. If empowerment is a stated objective of the assessment, then key informants may be part of the team for the entire exercise or at least for a period of time. Whatever is decided, team members must keep in mind that the key informants are important people to make sure the results of the assessment are carried out. They are also important to make sure that the assessment is not a single exercise but the beginning of an ongoing process of community involvement and commitment.

Working with key informants is one important way of generating information. However these are special people. We also will want to talk with people who do not have such wide views, but none the less, have important views. The techniques described in Chapters 3 and 4 can help generate this information, as well as provide opportunities for professionals to learn with and from local people.

We also need to remember that interviewing is only one method of getting information. We need to cross-check our information and add to it by collecting information on the same topic using other methods. For example, by doing systematic observations and using documents. Chapter 2 describes these methods.

FIGURE 31   Collecting information from key informants

5.7   Collecting the information

Once we have decided what information we need and how to get it we can begin our fieldwork. It is a good idea to do a 'pilot test' for half a day before we begin our work in earnest. A pilot test has the purpose of allowing us to try out the methods we have decided to use to generate information and see if we need to change anything. For example, it will give us an idea about how long our interviews take, or how long a mapping exercise is, and it will let us try out our communicating, listening and recording skills in a real life situation. To do a pilot test we need to involve local people who will not be part of the actual needs assessment.

If we use the more participatory techniques we must still be systematic in applying them. The key to a successful assessment is knowing which techniques to use and in which order. It also involves being able to adapt existing techniques and develop new techniques as you go along. When we are planning a needs assessment it is useful to list the topics which need to be explored and then write down the techniques which can be used to investigate each topic. An example is given below. This activity is best done during the training workshop by the team who are going to carry out the needs assessment.

Careful sequencing of techniques is important to ensure good results. As mentioned previously, techniques such as community mapping are particularly effective at the beginning of a needs assessment exercise. Other tools such as

---

PLA Process and Methods chart

Process	Methods
Identify problems	Pictures, mapping, role-plays, seasonal calendar, focus group, well-being ranking
Prioritise problems	Pair-wise ranking, matrix scoring
Identify causes and consequences	Flow-charts, role plays, trend lines
What have we done and what are we doing to solve our problems?	Venn diagrams, historical profiles, trend/time lines, maps/transects.
What more can we do?	Forum Theatre
Action planning	Preference matrix, Direct matrix ranking
Monitoring and evaluation	Impact diagrams, etc.

wealth or well-being ranking work better at a later stage, when the team have got to know the local people better and have built up the trust and rapport needed to enable an open discussion of more sensitive issues.

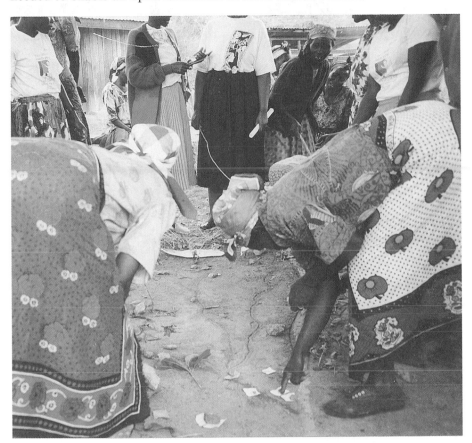

FIGURE 32   Generating information

5.8   Analysing the information

Most of the information collected during the assessment exercise will be qualitative. Chapter 2 section 2.9 discusses how to analyse qualitative information. The information pyramid is useful because it has already given us the main types or categories of information generated, such as community composition and community organisation.

To identify community problems we must start by comparing the information generated by using the different methods. For example, information from interviews can be compared with information from reviewing documents and from observations. If there are large differences in the information, the areas of these differences should be noted and a decision taken about how to find out which information is accurate. At this point the

From experience:

Needs assessment in Liverpool, England

A needs assessment exercise was undertaken by the South Sefton Health Authority in Liverpool, England. In this exercise the information pyramid was used to develop a checklist of questions to generate information on the specific areas in each of the blocks of the pyramid. Each of these blocks formed one of the categories into which the information from documents, interviews and observations was grouped. Information collected from documents was written in key words on yellow cards, from key informants on pink cards and from observations on green cards. Each card was then placed in the block on the pyramid to which it belonged. Using this approach, information sorting and interpretation took place at the same time.

team might decide to carry out a more detailed survey to confirm one set of findings. If we use the more participatory techniques, community members will be involved themselves in generating and interpreting the information as they develop and discuss their maps, diagrams and charts. This information and the interpretation is used by the team at each stage of the needs assessment process.

The second step is to summarise the information gathered in each of the blocks (categories) on the pyramid and write a short statement of the main findings. The whole team should discuss and agree these summaries. The summaries can then be grouped into the blocks on the pyramid. This interpretation can be the basis of a report, which the team will make on the information gathered.

The third step is to identify major problems. The team uses the findings from the information gathered, and also the experience and knowledge of the professionals present to make a list of problems that have been identified. This list may well include problems that the professionals identified but the community members did not. Whether these problems are important to community people is confirmed in the next step.

5.9   Reviewing the information with all needs assessment participants

The final step before we set priorities is to go back to the people who have been involved in the needs assessment and ask what priority they would give to each of the problems identified from interpreting the information. One way in which this can be done is to write each problem on a card and ask each person to sort the cards into the order of priority that they attach to the problems. If a problem that has been identified by the team is not seen as a problem for the community people it will be given low priority in this exercise.

From experience:

Needs assessment in Bangladesh

In Dhaka, Bangladesh, the team had interpreted the information they had collected and identified problems for squatter areas where they were doing the needs assessment. They arranged to return to the field to ask key informants to rank in order of priority the problems they had identified. Each key informant was given eight cards with a key word describing one problem on each card, and then asked to rank these cards in order of importance. Once all the key informants had ranked the problems each ranking was scored by giving a score of eight to the problem given top priority, a score of seven to the second priority, etc. so that every rank received a score proportional to its position. For each problem the average score of all the key informants was worked out to give an overall list of priorities based on the opinion of all key informants.

Once this information has been collected and interpreted the team is ready to return to the community to seek solutions to the problems that have been identified as top priority. During interviews community people will probably have identified some ideas about how to tackle the problems. In addition, various team members will also have ideas about what solutions are possible and what resources are available from their agencies to help solve the problems. The team, together with the community, must now decide which interventions they are prepared to undertake.

5.10 Defining priorities and developing a plan of action

There are several techniques which help us to define priorities. One technique that uses visualisations and thus provides a good participatory environment is a priority matrix. To use this matrix, the team has to decide what should be considered when choosing an intervention to improve the situation. For example, a possible programme to improve health status and encourage community involvement might consider the following questions:

Recommendation/innovation	Health benefit	Capacity for self/help participation	Sustainability	Equity	Cost	Time for benefit	Feasibility	Priority
Every house to have pit latrine built by family	+++	++	+++	+++	+	+	13	2
Provision of a health clinic	+++	++	+	++	+	+	10	3
Construct refuse bays and institute garbage collection	+++	+++	++	+++	+	+++	15	1

FIGURE 33 Example of a priority matrix to choose a health intervention

(*Source:* Adapted from Annett, H. and Rifkin, S. B., *Guidelines for rapid participatory appraisals to assess community health needs,* Geneva: WHO/SHS/DHS/95.8.)

- Health benefit (what is the overall health impact?)
- Community capacity (how committed is the community to solving the problems and what can they contribute to the solution?)
- Sustainability (can the intervention be maintained and at what cost?)
- Equity (which income groups are likely to benefit most?)
- Cost (what are the capital, recurrent and human resource costs?)
- Time for benefit (how long will it be before the changes are noticeable?)

Each possible programme is scored for feasibility by giving a + for low, ++ for medium and +++ for high. The highest total score is given the highest priority.

On the basis of this interpretation the team can draw up a plan of action. If we use the more participatory techniques then this plan of action can be drawn up together with members of the community. This action plan needs to list the activities to be carried out and set them into a realistic timetable. It also needs to show who is going to do the activities and what resources will be provided by the community and by the government/outside agencies. The team then decides how the results will be shared with the whole community and how to continue the partnership planning process in carrying out and monitoring the activities and evaluating what has been achieved.

Notes

1 Appendix 1 gives further readings on exploring attitudes and developing communication skills. Chapter 2 provides descriptions and exercises for using qualitative methods. Team members can also practise using some of the techniques we presented in Chapters 3 and 4.
2 The infant mortality rate is calculated as the number of children under one year of age who die for every thousand children born alive.

6 | Planning with partners: an example and challenges

This final chapter gives guidelines for using participatory methods and techniques in a practical situation. It gives an example of a participatory planning experience from Kenya, describing this experience step-by-step. In conclusion, reflecting on this experience and others described in earlier chapters of this book, it identifies major challenges facing professionals choosing to use a participatory approach to planning. It highlights the most important points for building long-term partnerships for planning programmes that can address the needs of poor and disadvantaged people in all parts of the world.

6.1 Doing participatory planning: an example

The example that we are going to describe was developed by GTZ (Deutsche Gesellschaft für Technische Zusammenarbeit) for the Kilifi District Development Programme, in Coast Province, Kenya. We have chosen to present this programme because it provides a step-by-step approach to building partnerships using the methods and techniques described in previous chapters. The approach is called Participatory Integrated Development (PID). It has the following aims:

- To start a participatory process for development which can continue over time by: 1) empowering community people to analyse their situation, develop a common vision of the future and make plans to achieve the goals identified in this vision, and 2) carrying out these plans and monitoring and evaluating the programme on a continual basis with very little support from outside agencies.
- To build the capacities of service providers (professionals) from various sectors to work with communities in a participatory way, based on the community's own demands.
- To enable the service providers to use the community's own vision and priorities in planning processes at all levels. (In the PID programmes this means working mainly with government officers, to respond to the community's own vision and support community development.)

124

To meet these aims, the process is done in five phases as shown in FIGURE 34.

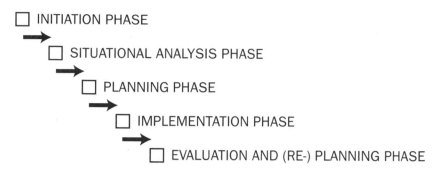

FIGURE 34   Five phases of participatory integrated development

Initiation phase

The aim of this phase is to introduce all potential stakeholders to the PID process and to select communities that are interested in supporting this approach. This initial phase takes about a month to complete.

To achieve this aim, members of a core team of professionals from different backgrounds run workshops to introduce the PID process to the staff of the agencies that provide community services, including government officers. These are the agencies that have the resources and technical expertise to support the development process. Members of the core team ask the agency staff to create teams of people from a wide range of sectors to facilitate the introduction of PID in specific communities. They discuss with the agency staff how financial support may be gained through their own efforts and from outside agencies. The core team also hold public meetings, make informal contacts and run training workshops for local leaders, who are responsible for discussing the PID process with their communities and helping them decide whether they want to be involved in it.

They then take applications from communities who want to join the PID process. Community leaders must present documented evidence that they have involved a cross-section of community people in deciding to apply – especially women and other less advantaged people. The PID team selects communities using a set of criteria the core team has developed, after visiting the communities and assessing their level of commitment to the process.

Situational analysis phase

The purpose of this phase is to help communities:

- identify important key elements of their current situation (for example, that they are an isolated rural community in the mountains with poor soil for farming),

- agree on their long-term goals or development priorities. (This provides a common vision of what they would like their community to be in 15-20 years.)
- increase their motivation to take responsibility for and ownership of their development process.

This phase has four steps. It is done through two workshops each lasting two to three days. This phase takes up to two months to complete.

Step One is to introduce the objectives of the workshop, which are to:
- bring together as many community members as possible to analyse their situation,
- agree on common goals for the community,
- plan concrete activities to reach these goals.

Step Two is to build strong links between the PID team and the community members.

During this phase, the team chooses the most appropriate method from those we have described in Chapters 2, 3 and 4 to help the team and community members become comfortable in working together. For example, the group can do a community walk and draw a *transect diagram* to examine community potentials and problems. They can also create a *drama* (role-play) to show the problems of dependency (relying on outside resources) rather than self-reliance (relying on themselves). At the end, the team presents an overview of the whole PID process so far, including the expected outcomes. They are strongly encouraged to use visualisation techniques.

From experience:

The River Code exercise

One drama that is used is called the River Code. It is used to illustrate self-reliance (independence) in development and to avoid dependency (reliance on outside resources). Three men and one woman are asked to volunteer for a role-play. After the facilitator has given them some instructions and they have had a chance to practise, they present this drama to the rest of the participants.

Here is the play:
A woman and two men are going to a wedding. They come to a river swollen by a storm. A man comes along and offers to carry them across on his shoulders. He carries the two men across in this way but the woman refuses to be carried because it is against her culture. The man offers to guide her across by holding her hand. She agrees and successfully crosses the river.

The groups together then consider the following questions:

- What did we see?
- What did we hear?
- Would we rather be the men who were carried across or the woman who was guided across? Why?
- What advice would we give to the strong man, to the men carried across and to the woman led across?
- Who do these people represent?
- Have we seen this kind of development in our community?
- Is this the kind of development we would like to have?

   In conclusion, the facilitator points out that for development to be both successful and long lasting, people need to take responsibility for their own progress. They should not rely on others to carry them across the river.

Step Three is to carry out a needs assessment to help the community to understand their present situation better using the methods we have already described in earlier chapters. This needs assessment answers the question 'Where are we now?

- A *social map* helps people understand the physical structure of the community, the different ways people make a living, and key issues facing the community.
- An *historical profile* helps community members look at the past and highlight issues that occur again and again.
- A *Venn diagram* helps to show the various organisations (or groups) that play an important role in community life and their relationship to each other.
- A *daily routine diagram* looks at the activities of various community groups over a 24-hour period. It helps to highlight differences between the workloads and income of young and old people and of men and women. This technique helps promote discussion about unequal distribution of labour and income between ages and sexes, which can continue throughout the planning process.

Step Four brings the information generated from the previous steps together into a so-called *visioning matrix* (see below). This matrix helps develop a community vision of the future. It identifies the actions that have been taken so far and further actions that need to be taken to realise this vision. The visioning matrix answers the question 'Where do we want to be?

Training exercise:

Visioning matrix

1 Divide participants into groups depending on their age and gender.
2 Explain that we will look at the past, present and future. The objective is to decide on what kind of future we want after reviewing the past and present, and identifying ongoing trends.
3 Ask the participants to 'brainstorm' (provide whatever idea first comes to their minds) on important aspects of life that they would like to investigate in depth. These topics should be fairly broad, such as environment, income generation, health, education opportunities, gender relations, etc.
4 Help the group to set up the matrix outline in five columns (aspect of life, past, present, probable future, preferred future).
5 After the group has filled in the boxes with the aspect of life, proceed through the matrix with the group describing how each aspect was in the past, how it will be in the future if present trends continue (probable future) and how participants would like it to be (preferred future).
6 Ask participants to identify the reasons for the trends – why have things changed? These can be important for identifying underlying causes and for planning strategies for improvement.
7 Discuss the links between the rows of the matrix; for example the relationship between population growth, poverty and income generation.
8 When the matrix is complete, consider with the participants how they can move from the present situation to the preferred future. If the probable future is negative, then discuss what can be done to move the situation to the preferred future. If the probable future is positive, then discuss how the positive trends can be continued and supported. It is not important to decide on details at this point.
9 Present, discuss and record the matrices. The discussion should focus on the common points and differences among the matrices. This discussion provides the basis for agreeing upon a long-term goal.
10 When the exercise is complete the group is asked how to move the matrix from the present situation to a future situation. If the future looks bleak (negative) the groups will need to identify which changes are necessary to make the future situation better (more positive). If the future looks good then the group must decide how this trend can be supported over time.

From experience:

This visioning matrix was developed for Kilifi District Development programme in Kenya.

Aspect	Past 20 years	Present	Probable (likely) future	Preferred future
• Commerce	• High-earning business • High value of money	• Low value of money	• There will be minimal business	• High-earning business be restored
• Availability of adequate water	• Many wet ponds and pans which could meet the annual demand	• Inadequate pans • Ponds dry up fast • Existing dams have been breached	• The community will be forced to get water from far off places as the population increases	• Adequate water available in the area
• Agriculture	• The area was fertile • Reliable rainfall	• Very poor farm yields and erratic rainfall	• Less farming activities	• Increased farming and abundant harvests
• Roads	• Were footpaths	• More motorable roads, though not maintained	• Will turn to footpaths again	• Graded and classified road networks
• Forests	• Abundant forest with hard wood	• Few areas are now forested	• The area will be bare and turn barren	• Re-forested areas
• Education	• No formal education in the areas	• There is a full primary school with teachers	• Improved education level • More children enrolling	• Improved schools • More enrolment • Improved quality of education
• Livestock	• Healthy and abundant livestock	• Few livestock • Poor health • Prevalent livestock diseases	• There might be no livestock in area	• Quality livestock in area
• Self-help groups	• Good co-operation among self-help groups	• Poor co-operation among self-help groups	• Many self-help groups will cease	• Strong and financially sound self-help groups

Aspect	Past 20 years	Present	Probable (likely) future	Probable future
• Health	• No adequate health facilities • Better health status	• Improved health services • Ill health	• Health status will deteriorate	• More improved health facilities • Better health status

FIGURE 35   A visioning matrix

This matrix can be expanded by asking the groups to draw a future map where the community draws what it wants to look like in 15-20 years. This starts the group discussing the environment and the physical infrastructure. It also focuses on improvements for social groups by asking questions such as: How do you want it to be for women, for young people, for the elderly?

The final part of this step is to agree some long-term goals. These goals are statements about the future condition of the community in 15-20 years. They can be stated in terms of the future condition of the community. For example 'access to quality education for all children in the community'; 'sufficient, clean water for domestic use within walking distance'; 'adequate fuel for cooking and building available'. These statements will be the basis of the next phase, the planning phase.

Planning phase

The key question for this phase of the participatory planning process is how to move from the present situation to the preferred future. In other words,

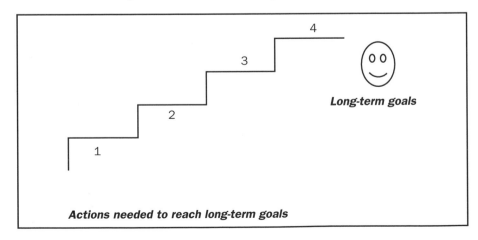

FIGURE 36   Actions to meet goals

how can the community achieve its long-term goals? What can they do for themselves and what help do they need from outsiders?

This planning phase answers the question 'How are we going to get there? It is likely to take one or two months and will include the creation and training of a community development committee.

Since these are long-term goals they are not very likely to be reached in a single step. A variety of actions over a long period of time will be needed. This is best illustrated by FIGURE 36.

Step One is to decide which actions, if chosen, will move the community closer to reaching their goals. The group can brainstorm to get as many ideas as possible. *Step Two* is to review all the ideas and decide on how easy they are to carry out. To do this the group can draw a *feasibility matrix*. An example of this matrix is given below. It has been developed using the following factors:

- Cost (least expensive).
- Time (shortest time to achieve).
- Need for external resources (needs little or no outside support).
- Sustainability (having the community manage on its own).
- Effectiveness (the most effective actions for achieving the goal).

In this example the matrix shows that the most feasible project is the hand pump project because it has gained a score of 14 points compared to only six points gained by the borehole and the dam-building projects.

From experience:

This matrix was developed to decide about how best to improve the water supply.

Criteria:	Low cost	Quick to implement	Little need for outside support	Easily managed and continued by the community	Total
Project:					
Borehole	1	2	1	2	6
Hand pump	3	4	3	4	14
Dam (built with machine)	1	1	2	2	6

FIGURE 37   A feasibility matrix

After a feasibility matrix has been completed and discussed, a community development committee is chosen. The community members agree on the way to select the committee and choose the committee members. The committee is responsible for writing the details of the action plan (as described below). The committee is also responsible for facilitating the PID process in the community in the future. The committee members receive training on their role as committee members, on project management, on planning techniques, and on getting support for the community action plan. Once they have gained these skills they draft the community action plan and present it to the rest of the community. The community action plan must show:

- The purpose of the plan.
- The specific activities to be done.
- Who is responsible for each activity.
- When the activities will be done.
- What resources are required.
- Where the resources will come from.
- The indicators of success for each activity.

Implementation phase

This phase is the one in which the community carries out the plan they have made. It requires considerable commitment, time and resources from community members. It is the most uncertain phase in the planning process and needs full support of the planning team. The time it takes to complete depends on the conditions in each individual community.

The phase has three activities that are ongoing and are carried out at regular times during this phase:

1 The first activity is organising the activities to which the community has agreed. This includes making sure that the materials and services are available for these activities. It needs continual follow up by the professionals and community development committee members to see that the people who have specific responsibilities carry out those responsibilities. It also means making sure that the resources needed are provided on time and in an efficient way.

   These activities should include some which can show success within a few months in order to encourage people to carry on with the programme.
2 The second activity is conducting regular meetings with the stakeholders (community members and service providers). These meetings allow committee members to review the PID process by looking at progress on the community action plans. At these meetings changes can be made to the action plans with the agreement of all concerned parties (including government officers and funding agencies). In addition, the committee should organise meetings at regular intervals for all community members to come to. These meetings can discuss the progress of the activities, how community contributions are being used and how much outside support

has been given. Such meetings are one way to promote community ownership and make sure that there is some community accountability (responsibility or answerability) for projects.

3 The third activity in this phase is following the progress of activities by keeping records and reporting to relevant stakeholders. Monitoring means reviewing the community action plans and also checking on the impact of the activities. By impact we mean how many people have been reached by the project and what changes have taken place. In this way, indicators can be developed to find out what the programme is achieving. Indicators are factors that show us how successful our activities are. For example, an indicator for a nutrition project may be '*By the end of one year 80% of mothers will be able to explain how to prepare oral rehydration solution and give it to children who have diarrhoea*'. Monitoring can also provide important information to the professionals and service providers. It allows them to put together a wide picture of what is happening in other communities that are using the PID process. An example of a monitoring form is shown below.

From experience:

Community Action Plan (CAP) Implementation Report

Community_____ Date_____

Date last visited_____

Number attending the meeting till end: Women: Men: Total:

Number of Project Committee
members attending: Women: Men: Total:

Number of PID team members attending:

Duration of Meeting .... hrs.

Rating (estimate of activity): A = very active; B = modestly active; C = inactive

Name of CAP project:

Progress reported on the project:

Progress observed on the project:

Plan deviations (changes to the CAP) and reasons:

Corrective action to be taken (if any):

FIGURE 38   Example of a monitoring form

At the end of the project, reports from the monitoring activities should be prepared to show the final result of the project. The community development committee, helped by the PID team or other professionals, should also prepare a final report.

Evaluation and (re-) planning phase

This phase can start after a number of community action plans are completed. This allows for the achievements of the programme to be judged in relation to the long-term goals identified in the visioning exercise. This phase answers the question 'How do we know when we have arrived? Based on these findings, new plans are made to reach goals that have not been achieved. If, based on the experience, the goals are found to be no longer valid then the goals can be changed and new plans can be developed to reach the revised goals.

From experience:

Digging boreholes in The Gambia

For example, in The Gambia community action plans were prepared to dig boreholes in a group of communities. The long-term goal was to release children from water collection so that they could go to school. However, an evaluation showed that when the boreholes were ready children were taken out of school by their parents to queue for water. This happened because it took longer to collect water from the new boreholes than the old wells. Based on these findings new plans had to be developed to achieve the long-term goal.

This evaluation and planning exercise takes about one and a half months but the timing depends on the nature of the plans. During this phase, the community is assessed by the professionals to see if it is ready to carry out its own planning without major support from the PID team. The entire phase could take between one and a half and two years. This phase proceeds in steps.

Step One is to collect the reviews of all the community action plans that have been completed and decide how well the communities have achieved their visions and goals. After this review, the community makes new action plans to reach goals that were not achieved. They follow the steps described above starting with the needs assessment.

Step Two is for the PID team to find out if the community is ready to use the PID process without much support from the team. The team will develop criteria for readiness that could include:

- The ability of the community development committee to carry out the community action plans well, with co-operation among members and with little outside help.
- The willingness of men and women to participate actively in regular community development meetings and to give good ideas to the discussions.
- The willingness of community members to take on the tasks needed to carry out the community action plans.
- The ability of the community to mobilise (gather together and use) its own resources and also to get hold of external resources to meet its long-term goals.
- The satisfaction of community members and the outside agencies with the accountability of the community development committee to the community and outside professionals.
- The ability of the community development committee to use PID tools to continue facilitating the PID process over time.

When these steps are completed, the community is seen as a 'graduate' of the PID process. The PID team continues to monitor the community's progress from time to time. It also gives support for difficult tasks, such as filling out forms for external funding, when the community development committee asks for help.

6.2   Identifying the challenges

In the introduction to this book we stated that:

> Information is **KNOWLEDGE**
>
> Knowledge is **POWER**
>
> Sharing knowledge is **EMPOWERMENT**

In the previous chapters we have shown how sharing information can form the basis of partnership by presenting a range of methods, exercises and experiences. However, using these approaches is no guarantee that information will lead to empowerment. The methods and exercises we have described do not, by themselves, lead to empowerment. Rather it is the attitudes and behaviours which we display as professionals that allow information to become empowering. Empowerment is a process of generating information and applying it for improvements. However, there is no blueprint for success. It is a long struggle to reach the twin objectives of information generation and empowerment. Experience of carrying out participatory planning has shown that as professionals we must recognise, and find ways of overcoming, a number of challenges in order to build successful partnerships for planning. In this section we have identified four sets of challenges. They are:

- Creating an atmosphere so that a wide range of community members can be included in the planning process.
- Being realistic about programme expectations.
- Involving local people as members of the planning team.
- Letting go of power and control over programme aims, activities and outcomes.

Creating an atmosphere so that a wide range of community members can be included in the planning process.

Communities are composed of a wide variety of people with various and often conflicting interests. In order for these different interests to be expressed and accommodated, it is important to build an environment that allows this to happen. We have discussed how this might be done in Chapter 2. Part of this environment is to create inspiration and encouragement to motivate people to join in the planning of a programme. To do this, we need to consider other demands on their time. For example, they might get paid for teaching adults to read rather than giving their time freely for needs assessment exercises.

In addition, we will need to convince all stakeholders of the potential of participatory approaches. Although many professionals may understand the benefits of participation, some of us may be reluctant to use it in programme planning. We may not have used participatory approaches before or believe that the approach works. Traditional attitudes and practices, whether they are those of professionals or local people, do not encourage participatory relations. As professionals, we often have to work within bureaucratic (administrative) structures and local people in hierarchical ones where some people have more power than others. Both structures support the development of formal relationships and obedience to people who have higher rank (not necessarily more knowledge and experience). We will need to make opportunities to introduce the idea of participatory planning to our colleagues. We will also need to be able to convince them that this approach is beneficial.

Being realistic about programme expectations.

We need to be realistic about our expectations, both in terms of setting objectives and judging successes of the programme. The aims that describe what the programme should achieve must be discussed and agreed by those providing resources (professionals and donor agencies) and the community who are intended to benefit from the programme. Sometimes there is a third agency involved that is providing money for a local agency to develop a programme. The partners may all agree, for example, on the aims of promoting participation and empowerment, but when it comes to deciding what approach to use for carrying out a planning exercise disagreements may emerge on how this is to be done. We need to be open and flexible to find ways of supporting partnerships and dealing with the wide range of concerns.

We also need to be clear about the benefits people will gain working with us and how we will judge their contribution. To do this, professionals and community people need to agree on community needs and criteria for evaluation. All too often professionals define needs based on their own experiences and evaluate programmes in terms of meeting these needs in a cost-effective way. Professionals often need to show in terms of numbers what improvement has taken place. Local people may assess improvement in terms of increased awareness and better opportunities – aspects of development that are hard to count. The building of agreement, confidence and respect among all those involved is why we pursue partnership. We need to remember this process is not a single act but the long-term growth of supportive relationships that develop over time.

Involving local people as members of the planning team.
It is easy to talk about the need to do this but not so easy actually to do it. In a typical planning exercise professionals from health, education, agriculture and community development may work together as a team to assess needs and prepare a plan to address the problems of poverty. These planners represent the agencies that will give financial and material support for the programmes.

Local people may not be included in this team because the planners may have already set the programme aims and have no time or interest in working with non-professionals to finish this task. But even when planners want to include community people in the assessment team this often does not happen. One reason is that it is difficult to find out who are the best community members to work with. For example, poor people often have no time or energy to take part in such exercises and local politicians, who may have time and energy, usually do not speak for the poorer members of their community. Another reason is that communities are often split by disagreements and different groups may not want to work together. To build partnerships, we must be committed to taking the time and trouble to work with local people. This is one way to ensure our aim of empowerment can be reached.

Letting go of power and control over programme aims, activities and outcomes.
By involving local people we, as professionals, are giving up complete power and control over the design and management of the programme. Many of us see this step as threatening and dangerous because we can no longer be sure that the programmes are making good use of the resources given to them. We may feel afraid that we will be challenged about the power given to local people if things go wrong. Past experiences, attitudes, beliefs and usually behaviours reinforce the power, high status and often the salaries of professionals. We may not want to share power with local people if this might damage our chances of continuing to receive these rewards. This is why, for example, medical people have often tried to stop lay people from being involved in giving basic health care.

From experience:

The community health worker

In the late 1970s and early 1980s, Community Health Worker (CHW) programmes were started by governments in Asia, Africa and Latin America. CHWs were chosen by local communities to give health care and health education to people in their community. They were given government support, a small amount of money and sometimes a basic first aid kit. Their potential contribution to improving community health was welcomed by both professionals and community people. However, there are almost no CHW programmes supported by a national government today. There are many reasons why they have disappeared. One major reason was that the medical profession in many countries thought these lay people were 'quacks' (no-use). Fully-qualified doctors looked down on them and this made them lose confidence. In countries like Colombia, it was suggested that they should become the lowest level workers in the health system and support the work of the doctors.

Partnership in part is about sharing power equally among all partners. As professionals, we need to learn to share power in order to strengthen the programmes. It is not an easy lesson to learn but it is vital if our objectives are to be reached.

6.3   Conclusion: Building successful partnerships

The planning exercise we presented at the start of this chapter is just one way of building partnerships, there are many others. Following the step-by-step guidelines we have described can help to make planning systematic but it is not guaranteed to build successful partnerships. Success depends on a number of other factors, which include overcoming the challenges described above and remembering the following issues.

Firstly, we must always remember that building partnerships is a process. While the outcome (such as better health and improved education) is important, it can only continue over time if the process has been carried out in a participatory way. The methods and techniques we have described can only help to support participation and partnership if they are used in a participatory way.

Secondly, as professionals and planners we need to be open and honest about our aims. We need to decide among ourselves how important we think it is to use participatory approaches to generate information that can lead to empowerment. If it is very important, we need to make sure that a participatory climate exists. (We have discussed how such an environment can be created in Chapter 1.) We also need to make sure that we have enough resources (especially time) to use these approaches and make useful opportunities for local partners to become empowered.

Thirdly, we must be willing and able to deal with disagreements. Participation is about power and control and building partnerships and, for the reasons we have outlined above, is bound to cause disagreements. In the past people have all too often tried to ignore differences. We need to build climates and develop skills, which will allow all those involved to discuss these disagreements with each other and overcome them.

FIGURE 39   Building partnerships

In conclusion, we know that building partnerships is a long and difficult process. It demands time, energy and commitment from both planners and beneficiaries of programmes. The methods and techniques we describe here are only as participatory as the attitudes and behaviours of the people who use them. There is no magic bullet called participation to make sure that poor people climb out of their poverty. There is only hard work and belief in the rights and ability of all people to share in the resources and processes that reduce poverty. *Partners in Planning* hopefully provides guidelines to help make lives better for people whose opportunities have been limited by history, ignorance and lack of concern.

Appendix 1: Further reading and select bibliography

Almedom, A., Blumenthal, U. and Manderson, L. (1997) *Hygiene Evaluation Procedures: Approaches and Methods for Assessing Water- and Sanitation-Related Hygiene Practices*, Boston, Ma: International Nutrition Foundation for Developing Countries (INDFDC).

Annett, H. and Rifkin, S.B. (1995) *Guidelines for Rapid Participatory Appraisal to Assess Community Health Needs*, Geneva: WHO/SHS/DHS/95.8.

Arnstein, S. (1969) 'A ladder of citizen participation', *American Institute of Planners Journal*, July, pp. 216-24.

Boal, A. (1979) *Theatre of the Oppressed*, (C.A. & M-O.L. McBride, Trans.), New York: Urizen Books, Inc. (Original work published 1974).

Chambers, R. (1981) 'Rapid rural appraisal: rationale and repertoire', Public Administration and Development, Vol. 1, pp. 95-106.

____, 1994a) 'The origins and practice of Participatory Rural Appraisal', *World Development*, Vol. 22, No. 10, pp 953-69.

____, (1994b) 'Participatory Rural Appraisal (PRA): Analysis of experience', *World Development*, Vol. 22, No. 9, pp. 1253-68.

____, (1994c) 'Participatory Rural Appraisal (PRA): Challenges, potentials and paradigm', *World Development*, Vol. 22, No. 10, pp. 1437-54.

____, (1997) *Whose Reality Counts?*, London: Intermediate Technology Publications.

Cornwall, A. (1992) 'Body Mapping in Health RRA/PRA'. *RRANotes No. 16*, p. 71.

____, (1996) 'Toward participatory practice: participatory rural appraisal (PRA)', in K. de Koning and M. Martin, *Participatory Research in Health*, London: Zed Books.

Cornwall, A. and Gaventa, J. (2000) 'From users and choosers to makers and shapers: repositioning participation in social policy', *IDS Bulletin*, Vol. 31, No. 4, pp.50-262.

Cresswell, J.W. (1994) *Research Design: Qualitative and Quantitative Apporoaches*, London: Sage.

Estrella, M., Blauert, J. and Capilan, D. (2000) *Learning from Change*, London: Intermediate Technology Publications.

Fals-Borda, O. and Rahman, A. (1991) *Action and Knowledge*, New York: Apex Press.

Freire, P. (1972) *Pedagogy of the Oppressed*, Harmondsworth: Penguin.

Feuerstein, M. T. (1986) *Partners in Evaluation*, London: Macmillan.

Gillies, P. (1997) 'Partnerships for health and the potential for social capital', *Paper presented at the 4th International Conference on Health Promotion*, organised by WHO in Jakarta, Indonesia.

Green, A. (1999) *An Introduction to Health Planning in Developing Countries*, Oxford: Oxford University Press.

Green, A., Rana, M., Ross, D. and Thunhurst, C. (1997) 'Health planning in Pakistan: a case study'. *International Journal of Health Planning and Management*, Vol. 12, No. 3, pp. 187-206.

Hope, A. and Timmel, S. (1995) *Training for Transformation*, Harare: Mambo Press.

Hudelson, P. (1994) *Qualitative Research for Health Programmes*, Geneva: WHO, WHO/MNH/PSF/94.3.

IIED (1992) *Input to Impact: PRA for ActionAid, The Gambia*, London: IIED.

Illich, I. (1971) *Deschooling Society*, London: Calder and Boyars.

Johnston, M.P. and Rifkin, S.B. (1987) *Health Care Together*, London: Macmillan.

Kane, E. (2000) *Participatory Research and Action: Flower, Weed, or Genetically Modified Monster?*, Massachusetts: Centre for International Studies, University of Massachusetts.

Kumar, S. (1996) *South-South Workshop on PRA: Attitudes and Behaviour*, Bangalore: Action Aid.

Lewin, K. (1946) 'Action Research and minority problems' in G.W. Lewin (ed.) *Resolving Social Conflicts; Selected Papers on Group Dynamics by Kurt Lewin* (1948), New York: Harper and Brothers.

Liefooghe, R., Michiels, N., Habib, S., Moran, B. and Munyck, A. de (1995) 'Perception and social consequences of tuberculosis: a focus group study of tuberculosis patients in Sialkot, Pakistan', *Social Science and Medicine*, Vol. 41, No. 12.

Maguire, P. (1987) *Participatory Research: A Feminist Approach*, Amherst, Ma.: Centre for International Education.

Maier, B., Gorgen, R., Kielmann, A.A., Diesfeld, H.J., Korte R., (1994) *Assessment of the District Health System Using Qualitative Methods*, London: Macmillan.

Marsden, D., Oakley, P. and Pratt, B. (1994) *Measuring the Process: Guidelines for Evaluating Social Development*, Oxford: INTRAC.

Oakley, P. (1989) *Community Involvement in Health Development*, Geneva: WHO.

Participation Group, The (2000) *Introduction to PRA and Health: A Reader*, Brighton: Institute of Development Studies, University of Sussex.

Patton, M.Q. (1990) *Qualitative Evaluation and Research Methods*, Second edition, London: Sage.

PLA Topic Packs, Sussex: Institute of Development Studies. *PRA Health Pack (1996); PRA Behaviour and Attitudes (1997); The Ship: Sexual Health Information Pack (1997); PRA Gender Pack (1997); An Introduction to Participatory Poverty Assessments (2000).*

PRA Notes, London: International Institute for Environment and

Development: No. 16 *Special Issue of Applications for Health* (July 1992); No. 25 *Children's Participation* (Feb. 1996); No. 29 *Performance and Participation* (June 1997); No.31 *Participatory Monitoring and Evaluation* (Feb. 1998); No. 37 *Sexual and Reproductive Health* (Feb. 2000); No. 38 *Participatory Processes in the North* (June 2000).

Pretty, J.N. (1994) 'Alternative systems of inquiry for a sustainable agriculture', *Institute of Development Studies Bulletin*, Vol. 25, No. 3, pp. 37-48.

Pretty J.N., Guijt I., Thompson, J. and Scoones, I. (1995) *Participatory Learning and Action: A Trainers' Guide*, London: IIED.

Pridmore, P. and Stephens, D. (2000) *Children as Partners for Health: A Critical Review of the Child-to-Child Approach*, London: Zed Books.

Pridmore, P. and Bendelow, G. (1995) 'Health images: exploring chidren's beliefs using the draw and write technique', *Heaith Education Journal*, Vol. 54, pp. 473-88.

Rifkin S.B. (1990) *Community Participation in Maternal and Child Health/Family Planning Programmes*, Geneva: WHO.

Rifkin S.B., Muller, F. and Bichmann, B. (1988) 'Primary health care: on measuring participation', *Social Science and Medicine*, Vol. 26, No. 9, pp. 931-40.

Shah, M., Kambou, S. and Monahan, B. (eds) (1999) *Embracing Participation in Development*, Atlanta: CARE.

Schmidt, D.H. and Rifkin, Susan B. (1996) 'Measuring participation: its use as a managerial tool for district planners based on a case study in Tanzania', *International Journal of Health Planning and Management*, Vol. 11, October-December.

Sen, A. (2000) *Development as Freedom*, Oxford: Oxford University Press.

Stone, L. and Campbell, J.G. (1984) 'The use and misuse of surveys in international development: an experiment from Nepal', *Human Organization*, Vol. 43, No. 1, pp. 27-37.

Tandon, R. (1996) 'The historical roots and contemporary tendencies in participatory research: Implications for health care' in de Koning, K. and Martin, M. (eds) *Participatory Research in Health*, London: Zed Books

Theis, J. and Grady, H. (1991) *Participatory Rapid Appraisal for Community Development: A Training Manual Based on Experiences in the Middle East and North Africa*, London: IIED.

Wallenstein, N. (1993) 'Empowerment and health: the theory and practice of community change', *Community Development Journal*, Vol. 28, No. 3, pp. 218-27.

Werner, D. and Bower, B. (1982) *Helping Health Workers Learn*, Palo Alto, CA: The Hesperian Foundation.

Westerby, M. and Sellers, T. (2000) Evaluating sexual health services in the UK: adapting participatory appraisal tools with young people and service providers, *PLA Notes*, No. 37, pp. 87-91.

Williams, D.T., Wetton, N. and Moon, A. (1989) *A Way In: Five Key Areas of Health Education*, London Health Education Authority.

World Bank (1996) *The World Bank Participation Sourcebook*, Washington, D.C.: The World Bank.

Appendix 2: Using the spidergram to measure participation

The spidergram has lines on which the participation in a programme can be measured in five key areas – needs assessment, leadership, organisation, resource mobilisation and management. We can use the spidergram to help us decide whether participation in each of these five areas is broad (mark 4 or 5) or narrow (mark 1 or 2). When the level of participation has been marked on each arm of the spidergram the marks can be joined up to show a spider web as shown in FIGURE 41. At a later stage of the programme the activity can be repeated to decide whether the level of participation has changed over time.

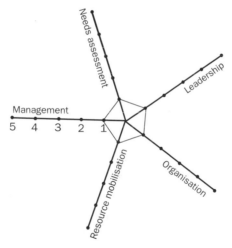

FIGURE 40   Participation viewed as a spidergram (Note: Marking begins at 1 as there is no community programme without some participation.)

From experience:

Assessing participation in Tanzania

A district health management team in Lushoto district, Tanzania wanted to know how much local participation there was in a health programme in one of the communities in their district. They decided to use the spidergram as a tool to help them conduct an exercise to measure the participation. This exercise was facilitated by an 'outside' development professional. It started with a four-day workshop to help the team understand the spidergram and develop skill in using it. The team then went to the community and interviewed 22 people and made observations to gather the information they needed. When this fieldwork had been done the team reviewed their information. Then they agreed where to put a mark on each of the five lines of the spidergram. They completed their diagram by joining up the marks on each arm to start a spiderweb. The results drawn on the spidergram showed that participation in the needs assessment was very broad. However, in the other areas (leadership, organisation, resource mobilisation and management) participation was quite narrow.

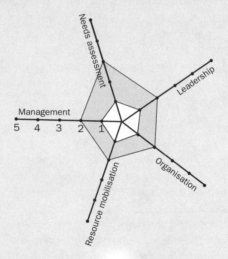

FIGURE 41   Measuring change in participation

When the team discussed their experience of using the spidergram as a tool for measuring participation they concluded that:

1 It gave individuals new insight about how co-operation took place in the community.
2 It provided a systematic collection of information on each of the five key areas on which future decisions could be based.
3 It helped clarify problems in participation in the community that the team 'felt' existed but which could not otherwise be documented.
4 It helped the team to clarify their own view of participation.
5 It promoted a good exchange of views between the team of government officials and the local people.

(*Source:* Adapted from Schmidt, D. H. and Rifkin, S.B. (1996) 'Measuring participation: its use as a managerial tool for district health planners based on a case study in Tanzania', *International Journal of Health Planning and Management*, Vol. 11, October-December, pp.345-58)

Training exercise:

Measuring participation using the spidergram

Purpose: To develop understanding and skill in using the spidergram as a tool to measure participation.

Time: One and a half hours.

Materials: Copies of the Primary Health Care programmes given in the case study from Peru in Appendix 3. Flipchart paper and thick pens.

Preparation: If possible, give a copy of the case study and the list of questions to each participant to read before the session. As the facilitator you will need to read this case study and also look at the spidergrams in FIGURES 40 and 41 which have been drawn to help you facilitate this training exercise.

Steps:
1 Explain the purpose of the session and using a blank sheet of flipchart show how to draw a spidergram, one step at a time. You can use FIGURE 40 above as a model and make your drawing as large as possible. Start by placing a large dot in the middle of the paper and then draw a line out from the centre to represent each of the five lines of the spidergram.
2 Explain that each of the five lines represents one of the five key areas in which we can measure participation – needs assessment, leadership, organisation, resource mobilisation and management. Label each of the lines.
3 Explain that each of the lines can be viewed as a continuum starting with narrow participation in the centre of the spidergram which gets broader as you move outwards towards the end of each arm. Explain that none of the key areas can be marked at zero because there is always some participation in the community.
4 Make points along each of the lines to divide them into five equal sections. Explain that we can use these five points as a scale to measure participation. For example, if we find that professionals are making most of the decisions and providing most of the resources then participation is narrow. But if local people are planning, implementing and evaluating the programme using the professionals as resources then participation is broad.
5 Take each of the five areas in turn and ask participants to brainstorm about questions to describe how narrow or broad participation is. For example, we need questions to show how:

- *needs assessment* is broad if local people do it and narrow if the professionals do it.
- *leadership* is broad if the community leaders show that they care about the entire community by stressing the needs of the poor, *leadership* is narrow if only the leaders' personnel needs are considered.
- *organisation* is broad if the programme is linked up with other community programmes and narrow if a new programme is started which is not linked up to existing programmes.
- *resource mobilisation* is broad if the community contributes money, materials and people, and narrow if all resources come from the outside agency.
- *management* is broad if the community manages the programme and narrow if professionals manage it.

6 Divide participants into small groups and ask each group to draw a large diagram of a spidergram on flipchart paper. Check that they have labelled each of the five lines and divided each axis into five sections to give a five-point scale.

7 Explain that they are going to measure the experience of participation given in the case study of the urban health programme in Peru. (If they were not given the case study to read in advance give them time to read it now.)

8 Suggest that they start by selecting one of the five lines and come to an agreement about how broad the participation is in this key area *at an early stage when the programme is just being started.* They should record their decision by making a mark on the scale from 1 (narrow) to 5 (broad). They should repeat this until a mark has been made on each of the five lines. Then they should draw a line to connect each of the five points they have made – to make the spider web.

9 Now ask each group to do this exercise again but this time they should come to an agreement about how broad the participation is in each of the five key areas *at a later stage when the programme has become established.*

10 Display all the spidergrams and ask each group in turn to explain their diagram. Lead a discussion to explore any major differences between the diagrams. Finally, ask people to compile their own criteria for defining how narrow or broad participation is – based on their own experience and the experience in the classroom.

Appendix 3: Case study of two Primary Health Care programmes in Peru[1]

Quispicanchis – A rural programme

The PHC programme in Quispicanchis Province, southern Peru started in 1974 in response to local demand. It was supported by the adult education school run by Jesuit priests, by the communities themselves and finally by the Ministry of Health. Funds came from foreign donor agencies and the Ministry of Health. Implementation took place in three phases. Phase One aimed to improve the performance of the dispensary attendants through better supervision and support. This had little success because the attendants had long settled into a routine of exploiting their clients. The second phase was to teach schoolteachers the principles of PHC. This failed because the teachers lacked the necessary commitment to help the local people. In Phase Three there was the training of health promoters selected by the community. This was later changed to include health training for groups of volunteers within the communities themselves.

The programme was developed through visits of the PHC team which had a doctor, a dentist, a nurse, two auxiliary nurses and eight dispensary attendants. The team visited 40 communities in five districts, selected because they were the most isolated and poorest communities. They provided curative services as well as support for programme activities. As the trips were long and arduous the team stayed overnight in the communities they visited. Through discussions during the long, cold evenings the health team came to understand better how local people perceived health and disease and the local people came to understand more about the biological and social causes of ill health.

Each community selected a candidate to be trained as a health promoter. Because the candidates selected had to be able to read and write women were virtually excluded. After training for two weeks and being given a manual that they had helped to compile, the health promoters began their work in the community. They started by giving simple curative care which was more acceptable to the people than advice on how to prevent ill health. They were able to use a stock of 12 basic drugs purchased by the community. The communities maintained strict control of drug supply, pricing and replenishment. A small charge was usually fixed for the services of the promoter but in some cases the promoter was exempted from communal work in return for providing patients with a free service.

A member of the team visited the community every month to supervise the promoter. This visit provided support and not just assessment of his performance. Every six weeks the promoters met as a group with the health staff to share experiences, improve knowledge and strengthen friendships. The team also encouraged supervision of the promoters by the community through village meetings to discuss topics such as the promoter's performance, effectiveness of the treatment, and the pricing and control of drug supplies.

The medical effectiveness of the PHC programme in Quispicanchis between 1974 and 1997 could not be evaluated because no reliable base-line data on sickness and death were available. Although the programme resulted in a greatly increased number of consultations (from nil in 1974 to18,000 in 1997) the referral system was under-utilised because local people distrusted state hospitals. Preventive and promotive activities had modest success but were not very widespread, did not concentrate on high-risk groups and failed to provide maternal services. The social effects of the programme were also unevenly spread. Health was discussed in many community meetings and many local people accepted biological and even social explanations for ill health. However, health promoters felt that they were unable to share their knowledge with the community so no 'ripple effect' occurred. Overall control of the programme was too firmly in the hands of the doctor in charge of the provincial health service, which caused dissatisfaction amongst some other health workers and created a sense of dependency on the doctor amongst the community. Involvement of local communities in the programme was generally limited to participating in programme activities. The programme was completely planned and managed by the health staff.

Villa el Salvador – an urban programme

Villa el Salvador is a slum area in Lima, capital of Peru. Privately-owned pharmacies and doctors' surgeries began operating soon after the people arrived in the area. At the same time the people began organising their own health care through regular meetings to discuss health problems. Many such meetings chose one person to be responsible for health care, starting with collecting basic drugs and organising the burning of rubbish. Funds were collected through Sunday dances and lotteries. The first of ten health committees was elected in 1971. These committees made records of the people living in the slum and helped with the government's mass immunisation campaign.

In 1973 the community formed its own development organisation known as CUAVES (Urban Community of Self-Sufficiency) which helped to organise a Primary Health Care programme and a community bank. This bank acted as a savings bank and a source of credit for community-owned enterprises such as a bakery. A new health plan for Villa el Salvador was drawn up by community leaders in discussion with doctors from the National University of San Marcos, and submitted to a general meeting of representatives from the whole community. This plan proposed that a health committee be set up consisting of elected representatives from each block of 300 families. Each block would also have a health promoter. The organisational centre of the programme would be a community pharmacy to be built by community members and paid for by the community bank.

The plan was approved and the pharmacy soon built. By1978 the pharmacy staff consisted of a permanent doctor assisted by various voluntary doctors and nurses and four health promoters receiving a small wage. The programme was carried out in the community by 60 health promoters, virtually all of them women, who understood the problems of inequality and injustice. About half the health promoters were politically motivated. One promoter commented 'I became a health promoter to help bring about a just community....In our block we have succeeded in having everyone pay for communal services according to their capacity'. Health promoters have weekly training sessions in the community pharmacy which include ongoing supervision through discussion of their activities. Nine traditional midwives have also been trained in the community pharmacy. However, the Ministry of Health has not adequately supported the CUAVES-sponsored health programme and has even opposed it in various ways. For example, when the health promoters identified 140 tuberculosis cases the Ministry did not send the free drugs the patients were entitled to receive.

The medical effectiveness of the programme is probably limited. The other main elements of the programme – health education, mother-and-child health, promotion of sanitation and health monitoring – have reached about 10 per cent of those needing them. The programme's main importance, however, is as an expression of popular concern about community health. It resulted originally from the people's efforts to overcome certain health problems. But, once created, it developed its own dynamic and helped the people towards a critical analysis of the reasons for their health problems. Health became one of the main themes of popular demands to the government authorities and other 'outside' bodies. The programme therefore had a much wider social impact than its limited medical effectiveness might suggest. Its replicability, however, is probably limited because few, if any, other slums in Lima have such strong, well-organised leadership. External support (in this case from the University Medical Faculty) may also not be available elsewhere.

Note

1 Adapted from Morley, D. Rohde, J. and Williams, G. (1983) *Practising Health for All*, Chapter 13, pp.191 – 207, Oxford: Oxford University Press.

Index